TO THE ONE I LOVE

by Christopher Hills

Edited by
Ann Ray and Norah Hills

UNIVERSITY OF THE TREES PRESS

TO THE ONE I LOVE
©Copyright 1984 by Christopher Hills

The author freely grants anyone the right to quote up to 200 words of text from this book without applying for specific permission, as long as proper credit is given.

Printed in the United States by: Fairfield Graphics

Library of Congress Cataloging in Publication Data

Hills, Christopher B.
    To the one I love.

    1. Meditations.   2. Hills, Christopher B.   I. Title.
BL624.H494   1984   291.4   84-11814
ISBN 0-916438-51-1

UNIVERSITY OF THE TREES PRESS
P.O. Box 66, 13165 Pine Street
Boulder Creek, California 95006

EDITOR'S NOTE

The author has poured his heart into this book for the sole purpose of sharing with others the kingdom that exists as a potential state within us all. He went in search of this experience and he walked India with a teacher who knew that this state cannot be found with the mind nor by any route that feels safe nor any way that we expect but only by the unexpected, unsafe, unprecedented, unritualized raw experience of the heart. From that deep ecstatic center where we are all one, a rare devotion that has nothing to do with rituals, emanates between the lines of these stories and poems. The editors feel honored to have worked on this book which is like no other book that Christopher Hills has written.

TABLE OF CONTENTS

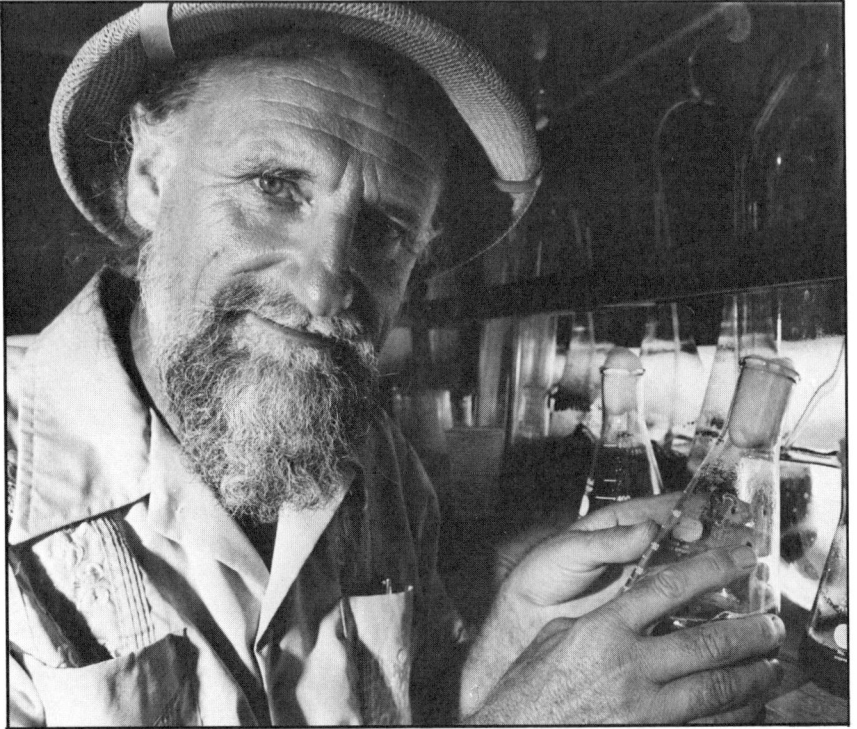

In the laboratory at Desert Hot Springs California, 1984. Here cultures of Spirulina plankton are refined and refined until totally pure. This is the first step in a dedicated research project to produce highly nutritious food that can be grown in all areas of the world to end hunger and malnutrition once and for all.

FROM THE AUTHOR

Both the poems and the true stories that you will read in this book, I wrote seven years ago in 1977. They were a labor of love, so much so that I felt somehow the time was not yet ripe for their publication. For me, they were like an indulgence—to sit in the backyard in the sun, writing what was so easy to write, basking in the love that was my inspiration. I knew that there were other books waiting to be written, books that would be harder for me to write. These were books with a message that people needed to hear but did not really want to hear, books written with a different kind of love, the kind of love that has to speak truth and take responsibility for the state of the world. So I put the poems and stories on the shelf for many years and did not publish them. Instead I published *Rise of the Phoenix* and *The Golden Egg*.

Now it is 1984. A small group of Christian ministers (particularly those called "fundamentalists") are opposing various aspects of my work. I am tempted to remind them that it was the religious professionals who crucified Christ 2000 years ago, but I have decided instead to publish this book, which they will understand even less than they understand *The Christ Book*, which I published in 1979.

Christ himself gave the teaching which underlies not only this book but scriptures throughout history in many parts of the world:

> *Then said Jesus unto them, When ye have lifted up the Son of man, then shall ye know that I am he, and that I do nothing of myself; but as my Father hath taught me, I speak these things.*
>
> John 8: 28

7

And Jesus said unto him, Why callest thou me good? None is good save one, that is, God.

Luke 18:19

I and my Father are one.

John 10: 30

Jesus answered them, Is it not written in your law, I said, Ye are gods?

John 10: 34

For I have not spoken of myself; but the Father which sent me, he gave me a commandment, what I should say, and what I should speak.

John 12: 49

Take no thought how or what ye shall speak; for it shall be given you in that same hour what ye shall speak. For it is not ye that speak, but the Spirit of your Father which speaketh in you.

Matthew 10:19-20

Neither pray I for these [12 disciples] alone, but for them also which shall believe on me through their word; that they all may be one; as thou, Father, art in me, and I in thee, that they also may be one in us: that the world may believe that thou hast sent me.

John 17: 20-21

What did he mean when he said, "I and my Father are one?" They crucified him for blasphemy, for saying he was God, but he never said he was God. He only said he was one with the Father, and he prayed that his disciples and others might also be in that state of oneness which he had experienced and tried to communicate.

This book is the communication of my own experience of oneness. Christ sacrificed himself consciously as an example of that state of consciousness by allowing the dogmatists to crucify him. He did not want to be made into a spiritual superstar or to be deified and worshipped. He wanted to be a clear window, a nothing, through which the light of the Father could be seen.

The spirit of oneness is visible only when a person is humble enough to get his own small identity and personality out of the way. It is a state that can be reached by spiritual growth that removes the fetters of ignorance from the mind. In the stories of my youth, which you will read in this book, you will see this process in action. For me, it happened in India, but it can happen to anyone at any time in any place. I left India in 1962, but it was ten years before I came to experience the oneness I believe Christ was talking about.

The gulf between man's truth and God's truth is narrowed by the practice of meditation, whether in the Western Christian tradition or by the yogic methods of the Orient. When I was in India, a group of fanatics planned to assassinate me. They felt that my book, *Christ-Yoga of Peace* compromised the sacred practice of yoga by linking it with Christ. In the West, some people felt that I tainted Christ by mentioning yoga. The word *yoga* in Sanskrit means "union," and Christ was in that state of oneness with the Father which all forms of yogic practice eventually reach.

There are many differences between East and West at the surface level of outward forms, but the Truth is one. There are as many yogis living the outward husk of their religion as there are Christians content with doctrinal concepts and afraid to penetrate to the depth of the cosmic mystery. The experience of "Self-realization" does not happen in the mind; it happens in the heart through an ever-expanding perception of Reality. No words written by me or by anyone else can give it to you, but they can inspire you to seek it, if you glimpse the truth that the One I love is you.

Christopher Hills

June 1984

WHEN THE CENTER IS STILL

When the center is still
the heart brings gratitude
for everything
because it is satisfied
with nothing,
and the heart pours out contented
thoughtless prayer
to the unvarying Being.
Ever-changing certainty
pervades the life
of the ONE who is stilled in joy.

When the center is still
there is no desire to move,
and all doing and work
is worship
to the ONE I love.

When the center is still,
the ultimate
all-aware
all-joy Being
of each individual
and of the universe,
stops all phenomena and time
and enters inside everything.

The ONE I love
is Truth personified,
the embodiment of Awareness,
love-crowned King
of all deep stillness.

When the center is still
the Self that sees is Pure Consciousness,
ultimate,
all-aware,
all-joy saturated Being,
melting the icy walls of all separation
from the ONE I love.
The ONE I love
is an infinite
ever-welling spring
of joy-saturated love,
the source of never-failing guidance,
the center of all-sweetening grace,
the stillness of the all-penetrating gaze.

When the center is still
the ultimate Being,
whose goal is the
gathering of all hearts,
guides us to the God of Supreme Joy.
For the gift of love
is given to every temple
and the joy of life
is hiding in every heart,
and the sacrifice of the selfless ONE
is seen in every Self.

Could I be found not willing
to work for such a wondrous ONE?
Could I begrudge the time
to sacrifice myself for love?
Could I be weighed on my own scales
and judged still wanting?
Could I be found out
by my own heart
to be unwilling?

MEDITATION

O eternal Master of the Universe
grant that I may be eligible in Thy sight
to penetrate your heart with your song.

Let me see with your love
and give love to all I see.

Let me hear the beat of your heart in all hearts
that I may be one with Thee in mind and body.

And bless me with awareness of happiness and sorrow
that I may understand Thy Way.

O Master Soul of all Being
grant me an insight every day
that I may sense with awe
the crystal clear Light of Thy Consciousness.

Let me see through your Cosmic eyes
the wonder of Thy heavenly skies.

Open fully my heart
that I may feel Thy presence
through the entirety of space
and be filled with Thy mercy and Thy grace.

O Great Cosmic Adorer of Thy children,
give Thy sons the power to adore Thee in Cosmic sound
and give them the Peace
which makes the world subside around
so that we may come to Thee
with clean hands and a beautiful face.

For although it is vain
to ask for what you have already given us,
it is in our adoration
that we would have more of Thy Being
and less of our earthly selves;
so that Thou, our own Immortal Illuminator,
may transfigure us with Thy Light.

Amen.

BEYOND THE STARS 1

Each star shines its rays through empty space in every direction. But space only seems empty; it is filled with invisible light. Consciousness and this all-pervading light are one and the same. This is the most profound mystery of all mysteries.

—Christopher Hills, 1984

I was standing on the roof of our house, built on the top of the Blue Mountains overlooking the vast city of twinkling lights that lay spread out before me. It was quiet time when the sun had set and the stars were emerging in the clear night sky. The whole of nature seemed to be in the magic grip of the witching hour as the celestial clock turned the evening into darkness.

My young son of six years old came up behind me quietly and stood by my side looking out at the vast scene of the earth below and the vault of heaven above. I began to wonder if he was looking at the same things and thinking the same thoughts as I was, for he was very quiet and I could feel the depths unfolding in his Being. It was a precious moment of silent communication.

Suddenly, out of the depths of the night sky he broke the silence. "Daddy, can I ask you a question which keeps worrying me and makes me feel very funny?"

"Of course, ask anything you like. It's best to get things off your mind," I replied. He paused a long time, trying to phrase his question. I began to think I had hurt him in some way or that I had overplayed my role as a strict father and he was going to voice some secret resentment.

The words came with shocking clarity and penetrated the depths of my ignorance. "Daddy, I am very worried. I have been looking at the stars for the last few nights out of my bedroom window. Every time I do it my mind goes travelling on between the stars to the space which is beyond them, and it goes on and on and I can't stop it because I want to know what is out there and where it all stops."

He paused while I looked out at the stars and went into the endless spaces between them into the infinite depths of the Cosmos, a place far beyond where I had been when he

16

asked his question. I stopped my relishing of the night sky and I marvelled that the child's mind and soul could journey into the depths of the never-ending unknown universe. I began to think, what child or even adult is thinking with such profundity at this moment of time among the four billion people of the planet earth?

He spoke again, more insistently, and with some urgency. "Daddy, it worries me terribly and my mind keeps nagging at this thought all day long. Every time someone mentions the word infinity it makes me shiver all over. Will you answer my question?"

I thought, how could I answer the unknown vastness so awesome that he had clued right into my own one unthinkable thought, the thought that dominated my youth, the thought that obsessed me as I walked up and down the bridge on the midnight watch as a young navigating officer, the thought that I knew no man had ever answered.

My son knew I could answer any question because I had an opinion on everything and had studied deeply all the books of man's knowledge searching out the deepest wisdom. But the encyclopedias in the head could not answer. The mind was impotent, an imposter who pretended to know it all. A child of six was making the books of the world and all the sciences of man into a heap of arrogant mental rubbish. What could I say? I paused for a time as I peered out into the empty spaces between the stars.

"Daddy, it frightens me and I can't sleep properly thinking about it, can't you tell me what is beyond all the stars?" I peered deeper into the vastness and threw myself into the depths of being. Was I going to say the usual answers to the searching light of the child mind? No one knows, I thought, can anyone know the answer to such an awesome thought?

17

Then suddenly the answer came out of the night sky and it was as awesome as the questioning mind itself. "All that is out there my son is the vastness of your greater Self. One day you will know that the consciousness which travels from inside you to the stars, between and beyond them, is the same One that contains all the stars." I felt as I spoke, how difficult to say to anyone what had flashed into my mind with such clarity. There was nothing out there except our own consciousness travelling endlessly— until we stopped thinking about it.

"Daddy, I am still frightened by it. Even if it is myself, because it is so big I can't think about infinity anymore." "Never mind," I said. "It may take some years before it becomes as clear as the space you are looking through. When you find the answer for yourself you will find yourself, out there beyond all the stars, waiting for you."

He was very silent and I could feel him looking into the depths of space with me, both together in the same place. In the vastness of space we were equal. We had become one. The six year old child was just as far ahead as the thirty year old man. The thirty year old man had just got the answer to the question he began asking himself at the age of six.

It was a profound moment and as I looked out over the lights of the city below me and at the sky around me and my mountain peak home, I knew I would be going to India and the East to find others who could confirm my answer. After all, I had to be certain and be sure, for my little son trusted me and I could not give him a false answer.

DUALITY

True love transcends longing and belonging.
In selfless love
there is no other to belong to.

To experience this in your head is one thing.
To experience this in your heart is another thing.
This does not make two things
but one fabric of experience
whose warp is knowledge
and whose woof is love itself
which interpenetrates all dreams
with its sometimes passionate
sometimes gentle
but always miraculous power to unite.

Yoga means the union of the many in the One.
But union is a foreign concept to the One.
Only two can unite.
Only separate things can unite.
What is already one unity cannot unite.
It just is.

The love beyond duality
is radiation without a radiator,
love without a lover,
knowing all things without a knower
because there isn't anything separate
to know.

How do we get into this inner space
where things are known
as we know ourself—
from within?

Make a sound.
Does it not disturb the silence?
When your consciousness is not disturbed
by external sounds or signals
you can experience the eternal silence.
That silence is the ground
in which all sound arises.
Without silence there can be no sound.
All vibration is the disturbance of silence.

How do we stop all the sounds
and discover the eternal silence
of pure consciousness at peace?
Can all sounds lose themselves
in the One, like a white hole in space?
When all signals merge
in the total sound of the universe,
the silence in which it vibrates
in our consciousness
becomes peaceful and undisturbed.
You are the silence of eternity.
But can you stop and listen?
Only the selfless and thoughtless
can hear the ultimate silence.
Can you stop your thoughts
and listen to the One?

Become totally silent within;
listen to your inner being.
You will quietly hear
the still small voice of your heart,
whispering in your inner ear
at the outer edge of consciousness.

This is the voice of God.
You will know this voice
whenever you begin to do God's will.

THE GREAT
CONJUNCTION

Stonehenge c. 1800-1400 B.C.

It was February of 1960 and in that year there was to be a great configuration of planets all lined up and supposedly pulling together by conjunction to bring about a new age. Predictions of astrologers did abound, together with theories of intergalactic happenings, the birth of new messiahs, and the launching of esoteric projects. I had just finished four years work on myself since retiring from business at the age of thirty to concentrate fully on my real life's work.

These four years had been full of discoveries including the fact that I was a latent psychic and hadn't known it and that by induction of various types of trance I could control the different energies of my emotions and the mind. After meditating in the Blue Mountains of Jamaica for all these years I encountered a businessman from Canada who was the head of the Seven Arts Studios which owned Music Corporation of America and various other interests. He had just concluded the contract for development of the island of Grand Bahama and its freeport.

After I had told him some of my ideas he offered me $25000 and, with my own choice of any site on the island, asked me to start a unique cultural center which would grow with the island's development. I had gone to look it over and do some bushing out of the land with a machete to get an idea of its potential. I chose the highest promontory on the land with the intention of building a Stonehenge type structure that would be seen for miles around.

The idea was to create a temple building with an environmental effect which would cause a polarity adjustment in the nervous system and bring about spontaneous healings, an idea that could be more easily grasped by visualizing Anton Mesmer's baguette. With bottles turned upside down to create magnetic domains, Mesmer filled a large round tub with iron filings and stuck rods into it. Patients were expected to hold these rods in order to capture animal magnetism which Mesmer believed was inside everything as a vital force. He was regarded as a quack, even though he was a fully qualified medical doctor and a brilliant student. Later it was discovered that this strange vital force was the power of self-suggestion sometimes called hypnotism by those who know little about the powers of mind. However, I was convinced there was something else which could be transferred from one person to another and I had set out to discover if the mesmeric effects of a "force" had been dismissed too early. With hypnotism it was said that twenty percent of people could not be hypnotised, but self-suggestion as it was known in India, worked with 100% of people. I spent four years researching this "vital force" believing that Mesmer had been grossly misunderstood by his contemporaries.

The Stonehenge healing temple which I had envisaged, however, was to be a much bigger affair. Stretching 100 feet across, the glass bottles were replaced with a quartz crystal floor with half the crystals' growing ends pointed upwards and half downwards in the form of a yin-yang sign. The upright columns of the Stonehenge structure and the lintels were built of small stones and rock formed around a hollow center and cemented together with transparent epoxy cement. The idea was that we would put up some sample columns and then appeal for visitors to bring a small stone with them from their home town and cement it into place themselves, locking their own "mana" or "prana" or spiritual vital force into the stones. In this way it would get slowly built by everyone who came.

The hollow centers of the upright columns and trilithons were to be filled with a core of several tons of antimony ore on half of one side, and the other half of the round building facing the sun would be filled with the element bismuth. We had found that we could make a huge psycho-

tronic generator by allowing the sun to heat the core of
bismuth in the rock. By letting the antimony remain
on the shady side we could create a vast spiritual
thermocouple which sent a charge of static electricity
across the building, stimulated the crystals, and psycho-
tronically charged up the nervous system whenever it was
out of balance. The idea was to simulate the radiesthesic
charge between the inner ring of blue stones of Stonehenge
and the red sarsen stones in the outer ring which the
ancient Druids knew about.

Also the building of new Stonehenge was to be orientated
to the stars and I spent some weeks with a sextant working
out the "Right Ascension" of various heavenly bodies on the
expected opening day and plotting the exact latitude and
longitude of the site from the stars. I was checking their
azimuths so that we could make identification marks
on the walls of the building showing where these stars
were when it was built.

The plans grew more elaborate day by day as various
people thought of different sound vibrations and colors
which should be included in the building. In the center
there was to be a radiating xenon arc lamp which duplicated
the sun's rays at all times and, like a lighthouse, sent
beams of color and ultra sound through the building. Also at
the center, placed around the light, we would put over one
hundred Tibetan dorjes which the lamas of Tibet had
brought out from their temples when they fled from the
Chinese soldiers. These dorjes had been chanted over by
very high monks for centuries and passed down from lama
to lama and each one represented hundreds of years of
vibrations of consciousness which were then expected
to be radiated out from the center of this rather grandiose
temple of culture. We had thought of everything except
the very gods themselves. The temple was to be the fore-
runner and pattern or prototype for healing temples

24

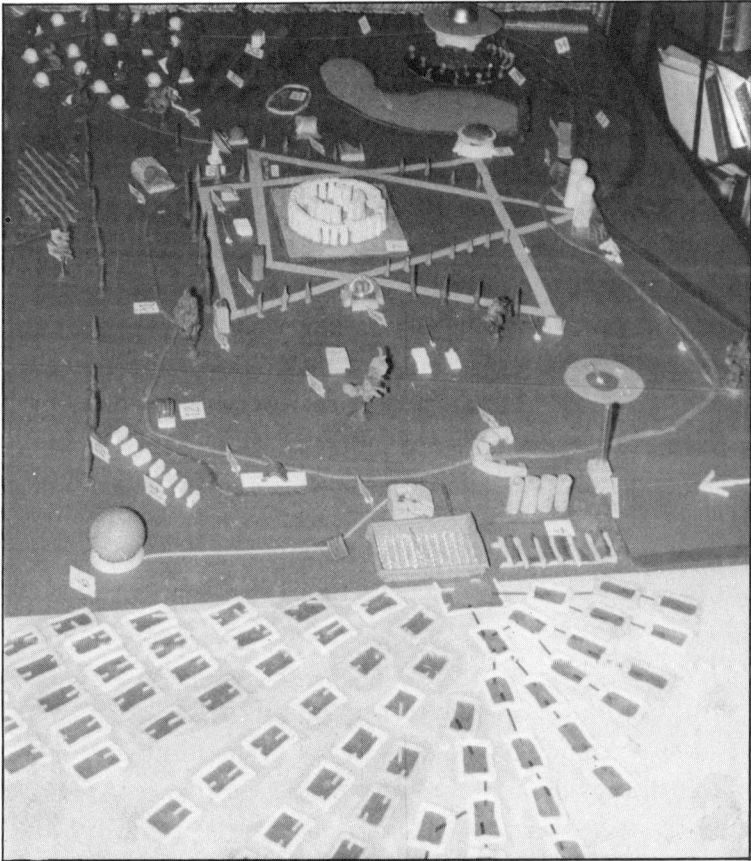

Model of healing temple, with ponds in the foreground by which the temple would be financed.

all around the world with all the latest scientific ingenuity of the age incorporated within its massive stones.

The Grand Bahama company appointed a famous TV personality as our public relations man and I went off to meet the multi-millionaire Wallace Groves who was masterminding the whole scheme. I found him very intellitent and sympathetic to some of the health concepts such as using an oxygen enhanced environment. But when I met the people who were putting in the big development money I did an instant aura reading and could see that they were not a bit interested in anything spiritual and were more concerned with getting a gambling casino started than an ultra-modern cultural center. So with a heavy heart after putting in so much energy, planning and work on the site, I reluctantly told my Canadian friend it would be no good if the policy of the whole operation was going to be set by the new financial parties in the project. Two weeks later he resigned from the project himself.

So I found myself on a Bahamian beach in Nassau with nothing to do. I was staying with friends at the Chelsea Pottery and on the night of February 4th I went alone down to the beach to observe the constellation of planets in conjunction. The western astrologers had all set the time at seven o'clock on the 4th but the Indian astrologers said that the great happening would be on the 3rd. I presumed that was because of their longitude being east of Greenwich meridian.

Arriving at the beach I noticed it was deserted and that people were all in their houses getting ready for cocktail hour as dusk was falling. I was a little early because I wanted to make sure that my calculations were correct. I had worked out that the conjunction would be in a certain part of the sky near some well-known stars and so I waited for the daylight to go away fully. I began to meditate on the beach about thirty or forty feet from the water's edge. I had brought some incense with me and stuck seven sticks in front of me in the sand and lit them. I pulled out my pocket Bible to read and see if there was anything in it about a new age beginning with a grouping of stars or planets.

I had begun reading the Bible when I noticed out of the corner of my eye a figure coming out of the water, still half immersed, and coming to the water's edge. I thought, "What a nuisance! I am not alone." So I put the tiny pocket Bible behind my back before he came out of the water, and waited for him to go past me.

Imagine my surprise when the man walked straight up to where I was sitting and stood before me. I felt annoyed. What did this fellow, who looked like a fisherman, want just as I was about to see the great conjunction which would not come again in my lifetime?

The man started to talk in native dialect, something incomprehensible about how he owed his brother ten shillings and I couldn't figure out whether he wanted to borrow some money or was asking me to give to him as a beggar. At that point I became very impatient because he was not only taking my attention off a very important occasion but I had just gone through this whole waste of energy on the Grand Bahama cultural center and I was now at a complete loss as to what to do next. Apart from some vague idea of a world mission I had no clear objective, so I was hoping to get a flash of inspiration at the exact moment when the conjunction lined up, at which time the pundits had said there would be the beginning of a new era for mankind. So I wanted to brush him away from the beach and reject him strongly and quickly in my anger at his impudence. A strange voice, which I recognized as my intuition, said inside me, "How can you be reading the

Bible one minute and then reject someone so quickly in the next?"

I still had the Bible behind my back as I was shy about reading it in public and did not want this uncouth character to know about it. I decided not to reject him but to give him the ten shillings to quickly get rid of him, when it seemed that on my thinking this thought his face changed from a rather nasty look of a beggar fisherman to a whimsical smile. At the same time I noticed suddenly that although he had just come fully clothed out of the sea just seconds before and I had watched him come out of the water with only half his torso showing, there was not one drop of water on his fisherman's dungarees. How strange, I thought, I must be seeing things, but before I could even work it out in my spinning computer he looked at me in a very piercing way as if he was saying something with a double meaning. "Why don't you forget the God behind you and look at the God in front of you?"

I was flabbergasted. Was he talking about the Bible in my hands behind my back? How could he have possibly seen from so far away before he even came out of the sea? Before I could even work out the significance of his strange statement, which was blowing my mind, he said, "I know why you are here."

I thought, "Oh no you don't; only God and I know what is going on in my life right now because I have not talked it over with anyone." I looked at him and said, "That is most unlikely, so why am I here?"

He looked up at the exact spot where I had calculated that the constellation of planets in conjunction was supposed to be. Then he slowly pointed into the sky and lined his finger up with his eye and said, "You are too late, it was last night."

Again I was totally bowled over. How could this being, whoever he was, know what was only in my mind and no where else? I looked more closely at him. Was this a real man standing there in the dusk of evening without any wet on his clothes after just emerging from the sea? I got the distinct impression that he was some kind of divine messenger and yet he looked as real as you and me. I looked at him absolutely speechless. Here was someone who knew not only what I was thinking but knew things I did not know, like that the Indian astrologers had been right.

He looked at me very intently now and repeated his words twice as if to get their meaning across, "The message is: Don't be too late, don't be too late." "Too late for what?" was my immediate thought, but as I was pondering the full significance of the words he turned and walked past me.

Now the dusk had fallen and the night was quite dark so that all the street lights at the edge of the beach were lit up. I turned and watched this strange man in his blue overall denims walk swiftly toward the lamps and was watching rather carefully to see which way he would go along the beach front road. He reached the road, then suddenly he walked under the full light of the street lamp about 70 feet away and disappeared right in front of my eyes.

I rubbed my eyes. Was I seeing straight? I was doubting my sanity. Had I seen a ghost or was there some part of my mind playing me tricks? I had had two experiences of ghosts before but this third one was very strange because it had brought me a special message. Not from the old God of tradition but from the one that is in front of my nose every day. What I was too late for I had no idea until I got home that night at the Chelsea Pottery.

At dinner we began to discuss the world situation and I mentioned my quandary. David Rawnsley, the Director, said,

"Well, since we are all stuck in our professions and jobs and are not free to bring about world government and universal order, why don't you travel round and find out what's really going on in the world and represent all the people who are not free to go on this world mission?"

I thought about it and said, "Yes, but what shall I actually do on this mission?" We decided what the world needed was a Framework for Unity, some book which would set out what the world was doing in the year 1960 to achieve universal government among the nations.

David threw a special farewell party for me a month later and I set off, armed with printed outlines, business cards and forms for completing lists of new age activities. By the time I arrived in India I had seen all the heads of departments of UNO in New York, UNESCO in Paris and FAO in Rome and interviewed hundreds of statesmen, leaders of movements, scientists on the brink of new discovery and just ordinary people all over Europe who were quietly working for human evolution. I was sending the materials to an editor in England who was condensing all the material for publication in the first volume of "Framework for Unity," a whole earth catalog of people working for the new age. But when I got to India I realized that this book would be out of date by the time it was printed. Again I had put so much effort into it and so had the editor. But something else was calling me. It was a Framework for Unity of another kind—Yoga.

For the next two years I became a sadhu and a renunciate and travelled India, Pakistan and the eastern countries looking for the holy grail and laying down the framework for unity with the One. Here I was, travelling through India on foot, on bullock cart, sometimes on the crowded train with nothing but the robes of an itinerant beggar to protect me from the boiling sun. Many times as I meditated on the temple steps of some fabulous temple I would remember the labor and effort and planning and most of all the opportunity to build my own temple on that far away Caribbean island. It all seemed like a dream. I would walk down to the Ganges near the burning ghats in Benaras and see the dead bodies arriving in their expensive shrouds and think of the dead projects and efforts of men, all dressed in the glitter of world glamor.

Where was that great spiritual guide to the world of 1960, the book which was to map out the state of the nations working for the new age? The Framework for Unity book had caused me to travel almost to every country of the world. It had caused me to expend thousands of dollars in air tickets and make hundreds of efforts, all to lead me into the life of a wandering mendicant sitting by the River Ganges watching the dead bodies come by and the living bodies go. "To what avail are the efforts of men?" I thought. In my meditation I saw the vision of Stonehenge in its prime and saw the temples of the world in all their finery and beauty. Yet the greatest temple of all, I had forgotten—my own body, the temple of the living god, not made by hands but by the Supreme One-without-a-second. Watching the dead bodies burn and smelling the strange acrid smoke of burning flesh and bone and hair, I knew that I had discovered the real temple and written the real book of the world into its living cells.

THE LORD OF THE BODY

It was said of old,
"Thou art **not** the body,"
but I say unto you that you **are** the body
and the spirit as well,
and when the Lord of the body
is sitting in his temple
he glorifies it
and makes it the instrument of worship.

It is a temple
which you build or destroy
with your thoughts,
and its architecture is patterned
in your consciousness.
When the consciousness is pure,
the divine architect sees no difference
between the body as the instrument of worship
and the worshipper
and the object of worship.

The divine incarnates in the flesh
and sings the hymn of great glory
in every molecule and cell.
Who shall say that thou art not the body?

It was said "Thou art not,"
because men thought the body
was all they were.
They could not bring the glory
into matter
and let it dwell in the body.
They could not let the light
shine like a torch from the eyes
and dwell in the heart of matter.

Yet every atom
does not pretend to be loftier than it is
while its heart is on fire in the nucleus.

What man is beyond the light of atoms
that give him birth?
What delusion disidentifies
with all that is?

For the great spirit is found
in the heart of all things
waiting to shine out of different eyes.

Great and holy is the instrument
that shines with fire of worship;
great and holy is the shining atom
that can make a humble body beautiful
with the light of all the worlds;
great and holy is the spirit of love
when the worshipped is united
with its instrument.

O lover of all worlds
lover of bodies and cells
shine out of your body
and worship with your eyes
the very ground you walk on.
Worship the consciousness
that sees into the heart of matter.
Call on us to feel your fire
and know the passion of your love.

AFGHANISTAN

CHINA

WEST PAKISTAN

PUNJAB

HIMALAYAS

TIBET

New Delhi

NEPAL

Brindaban

RAJASTHAN

River Ganges

Brahmaputra

Benares

Patna

GUJARAT

MADHYA
PRADESH

Bodi Gaya

BIHAR

Narbada   River

Calcutta

BURMA

Ranchi

MAHARASHTRA

ORISSA

Bombay

Godavari   River

ARABIAN SEA

BAY OF BENGAL

ANDHRA
PRADESH

Madras

Pondicherry

MADRAS

CEYLON

INDIAN OCEAN

India

THE
EXPECTED ONE

I went to pull the yogis out of their caves.

There was a well-worn path through the bushes and I followed it to the wall of the temple grounds. I walked up to the big iron door which was set into the hillside at the back of the Birla temple in New Delhi. This could not be the place I was looking for so I hunted all along the outer wall of the temple grounds but could not find any opening resembling a cave.

It was my second day in India and my friend, who was deputy leader of the Congress Party with Pandit Nehru, had told me that exact location of the guru's cave and it had to be here. I went back and looked at the door with a massive bolt across the front. No one could be in there I thought, because there were no windows in the side of the hill into which the temple wall was built. Another thought came—why not bang on the door and see if it opened? But how could a guru be bolted inside the mountain? Surely there would be people here waiting to see him.

I was about to turn and go away and ask for better instructions to find out where this radiant-looking guru was located and just from some impulse banged on the rusty heavy steel plate door to see what would happen. I was astonished to hear a voice say, "Come in." I looked at the heavy iron bolt on the outside of the door. Who could be locked in there? There was no padlock so I threw the bolt over and swung open the door which seemed to be so heavy but swung on well-oiled hinges. A shaft of light from the open doorway penetrated the darkness and gloom of the interior of what appeared to be a large room hewn out of the mountain side. There in the shaft of light against a wall sat a white-haired figure with his hands behind his neck in some strange posture.

I went inside and stood there as the yogi opened his eyes slowly and looked around, at the same time taking first his right arm and stretching it out at his side very slowly as though he was moving it after a long period of immobility. As the arm stretched I heard the distinct clanking of bones cracking at the joints. Then he slowly took his left arm and stretched that one out, again with several clanking sounds as the bones seemed to do some resettling into their sockets.

"Most disconcerting," I thought. It was more the sound one would expect to hear if someone was having his joints broken by some giant torturer. How bizarre! First a man bolted inside the dark interior of a mountain and now this spectacle like a traffic policeman signaling with mechanical arms which crunched as they moved. I looked at the man's face which had a blissful expression. Even in the half light of the darkened cave I could see a radiant aura surrounding this flowing-haired figure who looked like Moses descending from Mount Sinai.

He looked at me sweetly and said, "Everyone knows I meditate for four days without interruption, but today is a special day because I have been waiting for you." I noticed a strange light in his eyes. In the half light of the cave I saw his eyes actually radiating with a gleam I had not seen anywhere before. I was completely taken aback by his statement that he was waiting in this bolted up place of darkness just for me. I could not penetrate that gleam and found myself mumbling something about having such beautiful eyes.

He broke the silence and again I felt the shock of disbelief. "So you have come, my son," he said in a voice full of love, and charged with a sweet ambrosia.

"You were expecting me?" I asked rather doubtfully, since I was only just meeting him by chance.

"I have been waiting," he said.

There was a silence while I wondered why he had been specially waiting, when I had really come to see them all. I wanted to do the tour of the peaks, and ask each one of the holymen why they sat in the Himalayas while the world went headlong, fast, to destruction. I assumed that he told everyone who came that he had been waiting for them.

"Why do you say that you have been waiting for me?"

"Because you have to be recognized before you can do your work," he answered with a twinkle.

"How do you mean—recognized?"

"Well, how do you know you are the one unless someone other than yourself knows you are the one?"

"Are not all holymen the One?" I said.

"He who knows he is the One *does*," he said, meaning of course that their actions speak and there is no need for words. I thought for a moment. Was he referring to my secret thoughts, or was he just playing on a general theme which everyone would intepret in his own way?
"Why do you holymen sit in caves and on peaks if you are the ones who can solve the world's problems?"

He replied, "He who knows it is his job to act, knows he is the one, but he cannot be sure until someone who also is One recognizes it—that he is the one. That is why I wait for that one who knows he is the one—the doer. We who sit on mountain tops know we are not the one, but because we know that, we also know who *is* the one."

I was mystified by his ability to penetrate deeply into my psyche, for since early youth I had had this premonition like all youth, who eventually grow out of it, that my work was to be something special, that I was destined to fill the role of a world changer. These thoughts had always made me feel different, but I knew so many other people who felt the same; in fact, I had made a study of many psychotics who believed they were reincarnations of famous people. I knew so many resurrected Jesus Christs who were in lunatic asylums, whose messianic dreams had become a disease of the mind, that I was wary of the dangers of ego consciousness.

"You see, he said, "you cannot begin your real mission until you have confirmation of who you are by someone who knows. Masses of followers may acclaim you and boost the ego, but they can all be as deluded as yourself, with lunar madness. Such a validation is worthless. Confirmation must come from someone with the divine madness of John the Baptist." It was almost as if he were reading my thoughts. "Jesus had to be recognized and baptized, and you also will have to be validated from outside; otherwise you are just suffering from a crazy delusion, especially if you cannot manifest it other than in your own estimation."

I asked myself for a moment whether in my tussles with this Messianic feeling, I had overcome it, as I believed I had, in my four years' silent meditation. Here was someone capable of setting if off again, and feeding the ego. I knew so many holymen who got disciples by feeding their ego that I was distrustful. I had yet to know that I would come back to this holyman, and that we would travel India together. However, my distrust vanished when I saw the way he was looking at me with his misty eyes.

I replied, "You say I am the one, the Karma Yogi, but what about all those other men in Himalayan caves and peaks? I was going to visit them in order to tell them to get off their mountain tops and come to do a job of work."

"You are wasting your time travelling the Himalayas looking for wise men, if you *are* the one," he said. "If you can know me, you can know them all. We are all One," he said.

"Why do you sit on mountain tops then?" I asked.

"To carry through history the torch of a certain knowledge, to give to the one who knows he is the one," he replied.

"What is that knowledge?"

"That he is *really* who he thinks he is, that he is not deluded by Maya or illusion," he replied.

A sense of humility came over me. This cocky one who was going to tell all those high Yogis to get off their mountain peaks, seemed to have been melted by this old man with white flowing hair and his long beard. All I could think of was his eyes which shone now with a strange brilliance.

"And am I the one I think I am?" I asked, more to see what his answer would be.

"I saw you coming up the path, and knew you were the one," he paused, "Did I not say I had been waiting?"

How could he have seen me coming up the path if the great iron door had been closed and bolted from the outside? Was this man psychic? My mind began to twirl with thoughts. I looked at the contents of the cave. Almost nothing except a few milk sweets left by some devotee, and nothing of comfort. Even plates and clothes seemed to be nonexistent. What had this old man lived in the silence for? Just to pass on to me what I knew about myself already? Or perhaps I only knew half of it, until I had met him a few minutes before. It seemed impossible and incredible that a long chain of men would sit in caves in the deep silence of the

Himalayas for thousands of years just to pass on to people a subtle confirmation of their self-integration with the Cosmic Impulse. Was this the end of the path or the beginning?

POWER

All power is glorified in the One
because all power comes from the One.
All power returns to the One
because beyond the One there is no more.
Within the One there are no
separate dimensions because
all dimensions are universally present.

Power is the movement of unmanifest
potential energy, rising toward
its manifested state in our consciousness.
Power begins when the opposites resist,
yet, embraced in divine law,
move towards each other
to make them One.

The basis of power brings
the attraction of opposites in love,
and its agent is light.
And what is light but the marriage of forces?
The light force of the nucleus of the atom
which burns in the heart of the sun
is the love of its potential state,
the potency of its own manifestations.

Love and power rising together
are the beginning of the cosmos,
a relationship that ends
in the chemistry of matter.

Time begins when power
moves into love,
and life is born;
*but when power moves **without** love,*
disintegration occurs.
Solid matter annihilates, divides
and disappears in radiant energy
conquered by Light.

*Yet when power moves **with** love,*
the appearance of matter
brings forth embodiment,
the incarnation of God
and all the worlds,
crystallised energy of Light
imprisoned in created forms,
the incarnate light
which love will release.
*For love **is** incarnate light.*

Man is power gradually
disintegrating into death.
Until he speaks and thinks in light
his petty human power,
all bark, no bite,
is in effect
a lack of integrity
at the deepest level
of his being.
Only when his power
emerges from the One
and returns there in the form of gratitude,
is it infused with the creative ecstasy of love.

Though a man has faith and intellect
and understands all the mysteries,
if he does not love
then his understanding is wholly without wisdom,
and his faith is without value in the sight of God.

Power exercised without love is ugly;
crude expression compared to
power directed by love,
whose firm unyielding strength
is both graceful and patient.

Take power as your aim, like an arrow,
and make love your bow
to shoot straight at the many divisions
within the heart.
For it is through the single
heart that the universal One
will manifest as the power
and the glory
from age to age.

Love and Grace and Power are ultimately ONE.

TRANSCENDENTAL LOVE

He who puts light in the eyes
is your teacher and lover.

Learn from Him.
Love Him.

Through this you will transcend
not the limits of the known
but the limits of the unknown.

Life is both teacher and lover,
but in order to learn from love
you must have respect for the teacher.
The head is student of the heart,
but the heart is student of the One.

Is there a greater love
beyond what we have felt?
Is there yet a love,
pure, non-human,
independent and all-transcending?
Is love there whispering inaudibly,
unseeable to our human senses?

Why are the human senses and emotions
limited to narrow bands of experience
and who limits them thus?

By a thought
you can limit or delimit
all that flows into your consciousness.

Consciousness is not the knowledge,
not the experience
or anything acquired.
Consciousness is the knower of all.

How do you know what you know?
How do you know you are truly in love?
How do you know what you don't know?

Someday, love will clutch your heart
with its strength,
and waves of love
will sweep you with tenderness.

THE DOUBTER
AND THE DOUBT

I did not know then that we would walk the roads of India together.

"Why don't you come here to the Laxmi Narayan (Birla) Temple everyday when I begin to see people," the radiant guru said. But my mind went straight to the difficulty of getting a place to stay. I had arrived late last night from Persia and could not get a hotel because there was a big medical convention on in New Delhi. I had telephoned my political friend and slept the night on his verandah and I would have to spend some time finding a place before I knew where I would be or when I could come. My bags were still on the back porch of my friend's house in Janpath road.

"I am looking for a place to stay and then I will come," I said. But as if reading my thoughts he said, "Why don't you stay here?" I looked around the bare cave. Nothing on the floor and only a thin mat on which the guru was sitting against a bare wall on a raised up portion of the floor. No cushions or even the usual rattan web bedframe one could find all over India.

He caught my glance and said, "Oh, you are a visitor so you can stay in the comfortable guest quarters here at the Birla Temple."

I thought, "Who me? Stay at an Indian temple?" I did not know people could live on the grounds of temples.

"I will ask Mr. Birla myself as he always comes to see me at one o'clock in the afternoon," he said.

I felt a big sigh of relief. It was magical how things were happening. First I had arrived and had nowhere to go and then I remembered this friend whom I corresponded with about political philosophy. I phoned him up and went round only to find out that he was the deputy leader of The Congress Party and knew everybody. He gave me the name of this guru when I asked him for a list of holymen. Now this holyman says I can stay right here near his cave, right in the back wall of the children's playground behind the temple. I could not believe my good luck and really felt connected. I had not even been in India 12 hours. Wow! My second day in India and here I am a guest in a temple built by the millionaire Mr. Birla! Wow! How's that for good timing, I thought.

Little did I know then that I would sleep on many bare temple floors and meditate sitting up for hours on concrete without any cushions. I would sit with this guru until my soft bones began to hurt, just because this particular holyman never carried any bedding. This was long before the days of the jet set gurus who only stayed at Hilton hotels. Most travellers in India carry a bedroll even when visiting as a guest, so the luxury of a bed with a mattress on it at the Birla Temple was very misleading on my first day or two.

I was sharing the room with another westerner, an engineer who had given up his job and come to seek out the holy men of India. I was excited to know more about his travels. He said, "I came to this temple when I first arrived four years ago and this is my last place, because I am leaving in a couple of days to go back home."

Here was another stroke of luck, I thought. Someone who had done all the research already. Someone who had travelled four years the length and breadth of India. I was thrilled and hurriedly asked him for a list of the most advanced gurus, so that I could visit them as quickly as possible.

"You are wasting your time," he said. "I have visited them all and lived with them in their ashrams long enough to find them out."

"What do you mean?" I said, thinking he must have gone to the wrong places.

"All the great ones have gone. Maybe Ramana Maharshi was pure, but all the others are complete phonies." I looked at him and wondered about his perceptions because he seemed a very intelligent and discriminating fellow.

"They are just a bunch of blown-up egotists and their disciples are all liars who build up their gurus with stories to make themselves more interesting. I have tested them all and not one is without ego. Not one is without self-deception."

I said, "Why do you feel so bitter about not finding a good one?"

"There are no good ones I tell you! Just clever promoters who know the right words to say to flatter you and deceive you to become a disciple and work for them, so they can boost themselves in fame and get your money." He looked at me imploringly and said, "I don't want you to waste four years of your life as I did, always hoping to find a genuine guru. I am leaving, without finding even one that does not lack something, or wants something from me. I have been through the whole self-deception, serving them, while they eke out the platitudes you can read in any book of Sanskrit scriptures. This country is dead spiritually and as far as I am concerned, it is still coasting on the efforts of its great seers of the past centuries. There are no great men left here. I know! I have looked under every haystack, been everywhere, followed every possibility, done all they told me to do. They are charisma, just good hypnotists, able to fascinate the gullible and trade on the great spiritual thirst of people like me. You are better off leaving with me day after tomorrow to see some real Sufis in Persia."

"I have just come from Persia," I said, "but by a stroke of good luck I met someone today who is obviously a great guru right here on your doorstep. In the back of the Birla

Temple, behind a patch of bushes there is a pathway to a cave in the temple wall which has been shuttered with an iron door and inside there lives one of the most fantastic holymen I could ever meet."

I was now swelling with pride because not only could I tell him about the new find but I could also give him some addresses of Sufis in Persia. I felt already one of the privileged class, an authority who really knew a genuine guru. Just think of all those young people back home who would give their right arm to be in my enviable position! I savoured the situation mentally. Here was I, only one day in India, and he had set out four years before me and I was ahead of him. Bully for me! I was getting high just on knowing I had found what this guy had missed right under his nose. In a rather excited way I said to him, "Why don't you come with me tomorrow? I am going to see him and I will introduce you to the one genuine holyman left in the whole of India." And not a little puffed up with pride I added, "You see he knew I was coming and saw me coming up the path even through the closed steel door."

"Impossible," he replied. "They are all the same, with these words they delude people. How can you check that he doesn't say that to everyone? I have checked and found they give the same mantrams to everyone, and even say the same private things. They whisper to everyone words that can apply generally, just like astrologers in the west. You fell for it like everyone does. They make you feel special and you are then sold on them. But when you check, check, check, you find they are all phony. There is not one who can stand the test or deliver enlightenment."

I looked at him in his state of disillusion and in a rather patronizing way I was sorry for him. All these years wasted for which he had saved up his money and now he was going back to his old job completely convinced there was nothing holy about Indian holymen. In my next two years of travel as a sadhu and a mendicant travelling without possessions and absorbing the life of India, I was to agree with him many times and see the accuracy of his perceptions. But I was also to see life through the eyes of a great Being and walk the pilgrim's way with the one man he had not found. Little did I know it would take me several years to work out the meaning of the karma which had disillusioned him. For that moment I was convinced that I could be his savior and make his trip to India worth four years of his precious life. I would deliver what he could not find. I, the big Ego, would prove he was wrong and the conquering hero was right.

"What do you have to lose by coming?" I said, looking a bit superior.

"I am adamant because I know they are all phony when you test them. Most people will never test them or bother to prove their claims," he said.

"Well I have found one that radiates a certain light that you can actually see with your eyes, coming off his brow, even in the darkness of his cave. I have never met anyone like this guy. It is possible that you were destined to be led to him at the height of your own negativity, just to disprove your assumptions about there not being one who isn't phony."

I was feeling very pleased at myself for being able to help out this poor fellow traveller who had lost his way in the labyrinth of the heroic spiritual journey. He saw my determination and said, "I don't believe you have found who you think you have, but I will come, not only because you insist, but also because it's not more than 200 yards from where we are now. However, I think we are both

52

wasting our time. You will find this out when you get to know these fellows a little more closely."

I was thrilled that I was able to help him because I was convinced he would instantly recognize the difference between the holyman I had just met, and these many charlatans and fantastic actors who played the roles of teachers to millions of unsuspecting and devout people. Some of these men were even practicing magic tricks and sleight-of-hand that could put some of our western magicians in kindergarten school. Only that morning in the Indian bazaar, in the heart of old Delhi, a fakir had thrown me an orange and told me to catch it. I saw it travelling as an orange through the air and caught it in the open palm of my hand. When I looked at it sitting in my palm it had become a stone. I couldn't believe it, and instantly wanted to know how to do it.

"Is this real magic?" I asked. "Is it genuine materialization?"

He smiled knowingly. "Throw it back to me and watch carefully."

I threw the stone back and watched it go through the air to his hand. He held his hand out as soon as he caught it. It had become an orange again. I was determined to study this materialization process. It was one of the things I had come to India to find out.

I asked him again, "Is this real magic?"

Then he smiled at me knowingly. "It is a trick but I am not allowed to give you the secret," he said.

I began to think, "It's the same here as in England." I had taught my own children magic and then one day I had a house guest who was then International President of the Magic Circle. He showed my two boys things that I could not do. I asked him to show me the secret but he refused, saying that it is unwritten law that a magician never tells a nonprofessional how these things are done.

Here I was in India, with the same unwritten code. I offered to buy it from the smiling Indian. One hundred rupees, then a thousand rupees were refused with a strange movement of the head. I offered ten thousand rupees to see if his greed would loosen his tongue. He smiled, this time with an obvious look of contempt for such importuning.

"I told you," he said, "I am not allowed to give this secret. All our magic is hallucination, it is deflection of human consciousness. Go to the holymen if you want spiritual things."

So now I had found a genuine guru and he could see through steel and stone. I was convinced that this intelligent, young goodlooking man, my roommate, who so wanted to find the genuine and put it to the test, would be able to tell the difference between him and the fake gurus and phony actors that he had found all over India.

"When you see the genuine guru," I said, "you will instantly see what I am talking about. He is so full of wisdom that it is unmistakable. Tomorrow you will be convinced."

He looked at me pathetically. "I hope you're right," he said, "but if I don't think so and see that you are deluded, I shall walk out and go and do something else with my time."

"You will see that I am no fool myself," I said. "After all, I am not like you expecting to find many and becoming disillusioned. I came to India to drag them out of their ashrams and their Himalayan caves to save the world if they could."

"We shall know tomorrow which one of us is right," he said, and we turned in and went to sleep after a long day.

It was my second night in India and what had happened to me could only be real magic. During the night I dreamed that I was initiated by the new guru. The dream seemed very real to me. The next morning I awoke and looked around me. Was this a dream too? Was I really sleeping in Delhi's most famous Indian temple with all its ornate architecture surrounding me? Had I arrived at the end of my spiritual journey? I began to have doubts. Had I really discovered the great wise man of my dreams?

It would be another twelve years before I could fully accept that guru as my own Self. Unbeknown to me on that first day, I was yet to witness every bizarre waking dream recounted in this book.

A view of my room in the guest quarters of the Birla Temple.

WISDOM

What is wisdom but the rare insight
of simplicity
when one was expecting complexity;
corduroy where one was expecting satin;
frugality amidst wealth;
love where one is expecting thoughts;
peace where one expects excitement;
gentleness, which one was not expecting;
wrath which certainly does not fit
with a holy one;
clarity now or in a hundred years?

Thus do we recognize God
as Consciousness
and become the lover of wisdom.

Wisdom is merely removing ignorance
from consciousness.

Ignorance lacks discrimination
and hence lacks control
of the senses and emotions.
What does this mean?
It means that we believe our reality
and cling to it
no matter how painful.
In passionate love or hate
or ambitious desire, or lust
or greed or in impotent dreams,
life is pursued without wisdom.

Lack of control of emotion,
passions or body
leads to lack of tranquility.
Mind and thoughts disturb the peace.

Only rarely does the mind stop
for a split second of bliss
amid the tumult of pain
disguised as pleasure and gratified wishes.
Stop
for a second.
Peace is always there waiting.

To lack peace of mind is not wisdom.
To concentrate the yearning for wisdom
in tranquility and liberation—
that is the purpose of meditation.
Contemplation of the Divine Self
is the beginning of real Wisdom
for the individual life:
not sitting in a corner
waiting for something outer
to steal into the inner part of you
but rather just living and moving
and working and speaking and being
and feeling as though the skin had burst
and mixed the inner outer worlds
inextricably together.
Meditation is to let God
live life in you
while you live only for Him.

Renounce the fruit of all activity
and dedicate all efforts of action
to the God of inner tranquility and peace
to find the flowering of life.

Ignorance is the absence of tranquility,
while discrimination and wisdom choose
that which endures
through all impermanence and change.

To become wisdom is to live life
passionately in love with light.
To love light annihilates darkness.
The wise do not neglect darkness
because their business is its removal.
When ignorance and darkness are removed
then wisdom is realized automatically.
Realize consciousness and light as God
and wisdom will shine forth.
Tranquility of heart and righteous anger
are the hallmarks of a Christ—
wisdom personified.

THE ONE DISCIPLE 5

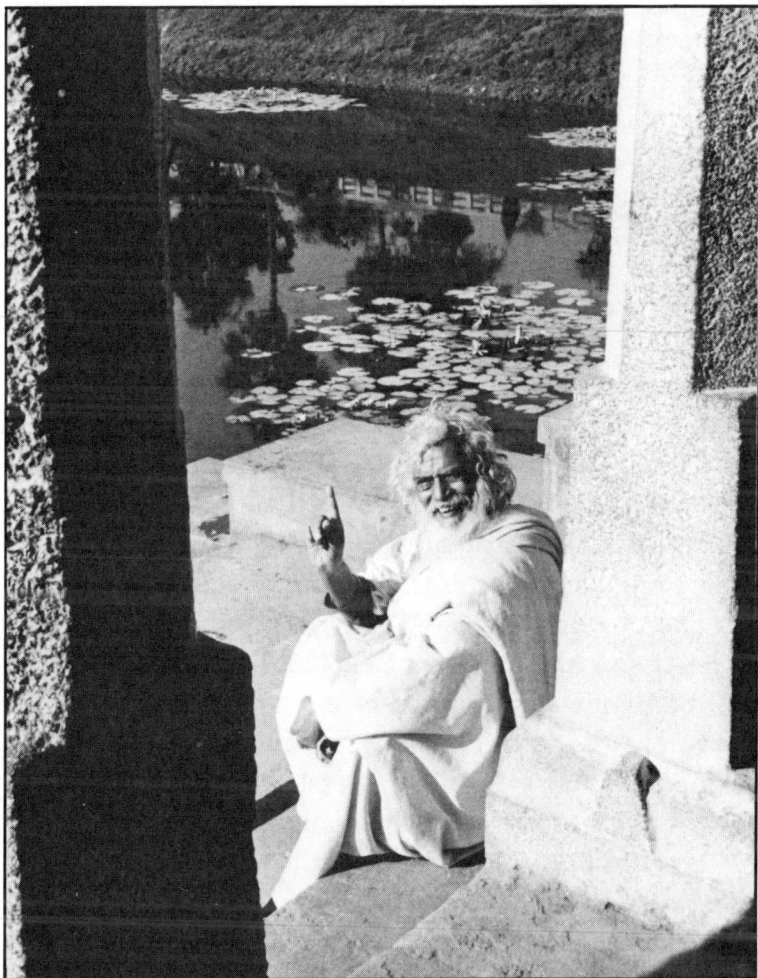

"I have only one disciple—my Self."

I woke up from my second night in India feeling that life was a dream. For some persons like myself the dreams come true and for some the dream seems to go from excited expectancy to disillusion, from wild hope and excitement to morbid thoughts of failure. I began to reflect on life at the prospect of meeting the holyman again. Life had been so full of action up to now, business, then research, then writing, then world travelling, and now the prospect of an exciting day hearing the purest wisdom flow from the mouth of a white-haired, carbon copy of the ideal mental picture of a guru. For others, life plodded in mediocre fashion through timeless boredom, occasionally relieved by the sensational dramas staged by politicians, actors, and the whole manu-factured public life of newspaper controversy, TV and radio.

My fellow guest at the Birla Temple was already up and about and seemed to be a part of the dream quality of my own experience. Four years serving gurus all over India and travelling to the next one whenever he heard there was a more genuine one to listen to, and still he had heard no wisdom, no spontaneous Truth that was in any way different from the spiritual platitudes which are heard as lipservice every day in India. Nearly every yogi seemed to say the obvious things—"You are not the body," "You are the Atman, the supreme Self," and such like—yet without any one appearing to be a bit supreme and all very much interested in things they put in and on the body, from food to beads. I could understand the skepticism my roommate was feeling, for I had come to India myself with that same doubt. Distrust had now been dispelled by the holyman who had been so genuinely full of love that I was instantly captivated and spiritually seduced. I was confident that his love was so obviously radiant that all the world could see it. I began to feel proud of my own perceptions. Proud that I had found in hours what others spent a lifetime looking for.

We walked along through the lovely ornamental garden at the back of the temple. Life-sized animals made of concrete which people could walk through were scattered among decorative pools with birds and the symbolic cobra snakes sculptured around them. Then came the children's play area made peaceful by the many games one could play with goddesses in the fine-granuled sand pits. Behind a group of ornamental bushes there was the gate to the pathway and sure enough the wall with the big iron door, this time wide open.

I led the way in, for was I not the one who had found the source, while my companion had been running around the spiritual supermarket? As I entered I noticed the place was crowded with all kinds of people: businessmen in western-style suits, a man who was introduced to me as the Planning Minister, the Director of Educational Services, and a whole group of government employees from Chief of Customs to judge.

It was difficult to find a place to sit, so people in the front moved forward and the back rows began to make space for us to sit. Because the place was small and lit only from the shaft of light from the doorway, it was a few moments before our eyes accommodated themselves from the brilliant sunlight outside to the scene before us. Obviously the holyman had been speaking because of the look of joy on everyone's faces. He must have stopped just as we walked through the door. The group had now shifted up and my roommate found a space at the back and just as I spied a place to sit, the guru, much to my surprise, beckoned me to come and sit alongside him on the little platform on which people had brought offerings of gulun japi and prasad prayer food.

I was instantly filled with a great feeling because I had been given a seat of honor alongside the guru facing all the audience and by turning my head I could see him deliver his words of wisdom to the disciples seated at his feet. After introductions of some other gurus from the south who said they had millions of disciples and had come to get the blessing of the great guru, I was even more proud to be in the presence of what I had come to believe was India's greatest man. Here was someone whom presidents and prime ministers and peasants alike adored as a great Being and I was very pleased with myself for coming straight to the top, in fact, I was just about gloating now that I was in the seat of honor.

I looked across at my roommate who had searched for four years to find this man as if to say, "You see, I told you, you will find what you came to India for." He looked back at me unimpressed and made a sign pointing to his mouth which was very clearly intended to mean, "Wait until the guy starts speaking the wisdom before I give my opinion." I remember noticing how good he was at this non-verbal communication and we seemed to have a good rapport which helped it.

Then the guru looked around and everyone fell silent as if they were waiting for pearls of wisdom to fall out of the air. It was obvious they were used to coming here and hearing the old man speak spontaneously. With great gestures the guru began to join words together in a strange fashion. Very clever, I thought. It would be very difficult to do this intentionally because the words sounded like he was making a speech but they made absolutely no sense. Some of the words were big and long, some were words very seldom used, as though the guru was reading a dictionary or the encyclopedia backwards.

How strange, I thought, and I looked around at the faces. Most were seated on the floor with eyes closed concentrating with a blissful look on their faces. What could they be hearing? What was being said was like intelligent nonsense. It seemed that they were used to this sort of thing, or was he doing it for some reason unknown to me?

I looked across at my friend and roommate and caught him looking at me very intently. The non-verbal communication was strong. He was saying mentally, "I told you so, they are all phony." I signalled him to remain seated and he signalled me that he had had enough of this nonsense and was about to leave.

I felt desperately embarrassed. I could not understand the situation. Yesterday the guru was a mine of wisdom. Today it was getting ludicrous as with every word uttered it became more obvious that he was talking utter nonsense. I signalled to my friend at the back of the cave to wait a while, so he sat down again. I indicated the wisdom would soon flow but I was feeling terribly embarrassed because the guy was getting very antsy and kept looking at the door as if to say, "I can't stand one more minute of this, why don't you leave?" I think he was only waiting for me to see the obvious so we could leave together and he could tell me he had been dead right about how I had fallen for all these sweet words.

After five more minutes my roommate got slowly to his feet and began to pick his way through the seated bodies to the door. He waved for me to come and not waste any more time. I could not believe it. I had definitely heard this guru spout wisdom and the whole scene was now like a dream again as the nonsense became worse and worse like some great clown at a circus, with gesticulations which had nothing to do with the words. My friend paused at the door and made one last appeal for me not to waste one more minute of my time here sitting on the right hand of a cosmic clown.

Just as he was about to turn on his heel and leave, the guru stopped suddenly and shouted, "Hey young man, come here," and he held his hand out with some white sweetmeat in it saying, "Come, I never allow anyone to leave without giving them something."

Now the roommate was embarrassed, for he had to slowly step through in between a crush of people to receive the symbolic gift and blessing. I could see he was tempted to reject the gift and stalk off into the world and never come back. But somehow he realized that would be an insult to the culture he knew so well and would leave a nasty taste with all who were seated there. I saw him hestitate for a moment debating whether to do it.

The guru called out again, "Come, let me give you something. You cannot leave me and take away nothing." I remember thinking that was either a mistake in English or a very good pun about taking away nothing, as if anyone could take nothing, but I couldn't be sure the guru meant it that way.

My roommate sheepishly collected the prasad and picked his way back to the door in silence. The guru looked at me very significantly, but the inscrutable look did not tell me what he was thinking. I was too embarrassed and humiliated, having promised my roommate the whole of heaven and delivered nothing but a clown. There must be some reason, I thought, why he is doing this. Is it just to embarrass me because of my pride, or did he want to get rid of the young man by this method? What was he trying to teach?

As the young man's back was out of the door the guru raised his hand high in the air and snapped his fingers and

I got the impression he was clicking some cosmic switch situated somewhere just above his head. A most bizarre action, I thought. Then it flowed. The young man could not have been yet ten feet from the doorway and pure wisdom had begun to flow and even in the first sentence I recognized the man who had spoken yesterday, and not only that but this time every word rhymed or alliterated. The sentences all ended in words with double meanings and the content was so profound that I could never have written it down or even remembered how to do it. I was flabbergasted and the great temptation was to run after my roommate and drag him back in to hear the wisdom. At least it would repair my broken image with him but the wisdom held me and ruled over all thoughts of disappointment. I stayed on and on and the flow never stopped. He was talking about everything in a high transcendental poetry—the world situation, the cure for it, the real message of the universe, all in language I could never have repeated or remembered because it was like trying to remember a poem after the first reading.

I was sorry and glad at the same time. Glad that I had been right about the guru but sorry the other guy had really missed out. I tried to puzzle it out afterwards. What was the purpose? "Ah, yes," I thought. "The guru knew the guy was arrogant and decided to teach him a lesson. He missed out because of his judgement."

Needless to say, when I returned to the Birla Temple guest quarters that evening my roommate had gone. Resting on my bed was a note from him. "We are obviously not of the same viewpoint or temperament. You were so obviously wrong about that guru and completely taken in by his nonsense. I am sickened by the whole scene here and decided to leave a day earlier. I don't think our tracks will cross again. But, best of luck! Thanks for trying!"

Many years after, I realized that the guru did not teach him a lesson, because my roommate never knew what he missed. The guru had merely used the situation, my own pride, the roommate's ignorance, the sitting of me on his right hand, the withholding of the wisdom until the reception attitude was right, all these things were done to give *me* a lesson. The young man had left with what he expected, the people listening got what they wanted, and I had been given the lesson I needed in spiritual pride.

In the two years to come I was to find that whenever I boasted about the Guru to others, or became proud of his exploits, which were many, he would do something which would absolutely embarrass me. On these occasions I would feel like I was naive and stupid to invest so much pride in one person and I began to realize he was teaching me a lot about ego food. How proud we are to have the best miracle man! How our own ego swells when we say our guru is so and so.

The Guru operated so subtly to prevent and counteract my using the current method of telling the usual anecdotal guru story. For twelve years I was unable to speak about our life together, without my feeling that I was tripping on the glamor and fascination of stories, rather than teaching the real message. I never heard him mention his own guru but referred only to the One who is in all. Many people have begged me in lectures to talk of my personal life and particularly life as a sannyasin walking the humble earth with a great Guru by my side. A reluctance is still there. I don't want to create a personality cult or get into the glamor of guru worship. This teaching which I continue is that there is only One who is your master. The Guru never failed to repeat that he only had one disciple—Himself. When there is only One, all selves are yourself.

THE ONE

Guru is the bird on wing
whose flight path traces
the calligraphy of heaven in air.

The good guru's goal
is to give the student his own grace.

All supreme gurus are ONE
with only one disciple,
the Self.
No other one to guide, but Self.
No other to love but the One,
for in oneness there is no self sense,
no otherness or "I"ness to separate
a second self.

The One is always giving
its priceless gift to itself.
This is the primordial purpose
of all existence.

This splendor cannot be got from guru
but only from the Self.
But from guru
comes the portrait
painted in flesh,
as the divine artist
strains the limits of his medium.

Guru is you,
now,
in this moment,
masquerading as a person
who is separate,
more evolved,
more wise.

It is this which permits you to trust totally,
for you will surrender ultimately
to no one but yourself.

Those who love the false guru
have a need
to love something higher than themselves.
When you love the true guru,
you do so because he **is** yourself.
He knows from inside
what you feel,
and this supreme love
is too much.
You cannot cope with it.
There is no time in which to decide
how much of it is prudent to return.
Before you know it,
you've given it all.
Like a flash flood,
your love sweeps through the valley,
uprooting everything in sight,
tearing down fences,
leaving the landscape
a totally unfamiliar place.
Do not try to shut it off
or contain it.
The guru is only using
the tools of his trade.
It is his job
to get behind all masks and defenses.
The real guru smiles innocently
as if he has done nothing,
for he has no disciples,
only ONE.

THE HEART

The heart which speaks its love
is not the real heart.
The heart that asks the questions
is not the constant heart which loves.
If you would know the real heart
do not speak.
If you would know the constant love
do not ask questions,
but open your ears and eyes
and learn its secrets directly.

For if you are speaking
you are not listening,
and if your mind is
looking at the problem question
you are not seeing
the gateway to the heart.

The heart is humble and empty,
therefore it can only be raised up
and made full by love.
If the head speaks for the heart
it speaks with pride of its cleverness
If the head sees for the heart
it looks at emptiness.

The head cannot tolerate
what is empty
and must fill it with speech,
but such speech is empty
and meaningless
because its sole purpose
is to kill the silence.

The heart which speaks its love
cannot listen to its silence.
The heart that asks the questions
cannot sit in its stillness.

Yet it is in the silence
and in the quiet stillness
that the heart hears its own voice
and knows real love.

INNER TRUTH

I looked across at his shining face and thought, "If you are my real Guru how do I know it?" I wondered if he was the highest one I would ever meet and whether I should keep looking. He turned his head and looked at me in a strange way with a hint of hurt in his eyes as if to say, "Why do you not see all of me?"

I asked a mental question of my inner mind and wished I could ask it of him. He looked away at the rest of the small group sitting around and began to speak impersonally about Inner Truth. Gradually I realized that he was answering everything that had been secretly in my inner thoughts. He glanced at me with a great love shining from his eyes and began to chant softly these words:

> *Truth is all one*
> *and truth is all there is,*
> *for all existence is truth,*
> *the total intelligence of the all-wise.*
> *All life is love,*
> *for outside of truth*
> *there is no life nor love.*
> *Truth is the power and the glory,*
> *shining for ever and ever*
> *through the all-loving Being.*
> *It is this Truth*
> *that is seeing from the heart of all*
> *in the light of our consciousness.*
> *Truth is all that,*
> *and without truth, nothing can be.*
> *All that is truth*
> *radiating the One I love.*

A CHALLENGE FOR THE GURU

A student spoke up and said to him, "How come you have all these important people sitting at your feet in very humble fashion?" Some were ministers of government and two or three of them were gurus with several million disciples. "How come that you tell important people to sit at the back and when a peasant or ordinary person comes in you beckon him to the front seat?"

The teacher smiled tolerantly but did not say anything. The silence was unbearable until the student began to justify his question. "I would like to know why you do not recognize the achievements of these pesonalities, and favor the ones who amount to nothing, have achieved nothing and can offer you nothing." The teacher smiled sweetly and cast a knowing look at me and said: "How many times have I told you I have only one disciple? Those who have millions of disciples are myself and if they come before me humbly how can I refuse their gift of Self? Pride, achievements and fame and numbers of disciples are of no attraction to God, who goes direct into the humble body of all persons. God does not come to the Prime Minister and President. President and Prime Minister must come to God. But when the humble peasant comes with nothing to offer but his heart and surrenders his most precious life before God, does not God come running to lift him up? When the humble peasant offers himself he offers all. When the proud and powerful come they expect special treatment. According to custom the important should be first. But according to God humility is first. Therefore I have only one disciple, my Self. This keeps me humble so I can adore those who need to be lifted up." I began to marvel as I watched the heads of the important gurus and ministers nodding in agreement from the back row of the small cave where we were crowded listening to this extra-ordinary man. With his blue eyes emanating his all penetrating gaze, my thoughts began to race. He opened up a flood of ideas and almost as if the teacher was speaking inside my mind, I reached for an invisible pen and wrote them in my heart and burned them into my brain with love.

The Guru outside his cave at the Birla Temple in New Delhi.

HUMILITY

Humility is valued only by the humble.
The self-important have no use for it.
To push, to strive,
to succeed and yet have
humility and gentleness,
is difficult.
Yet to strive for humility
if one does not have it,
is even more difficult.
For a man can only be humble
if he is so in his heart.

Humility is often forced upon men and women,
and ultimately death can be humbling to the mighty.
But to the humble,
being close to the soil by choice in life
will make humiliation impossible.

Proud people take their vanity
and flaunt it in society
as an asset.
Humble people take their humility
and wish they could be
more aggressive.
The proud are puffed up
and cannot worship the humble soil,
while the humble come to earth
to learn of life's lessons.
Both return to the soil regardless!

Look around you at the human world.
What is the rarest quality among men?
Is it not humility and the absence of vanity?
Where are the egoless even among the saints?

Though every baby may come into this world
without ego,
to depart without one is rare.
To work for this state
is a greater work
than all the world conquered.

If the good of men is buried
with their bones
and the evil lives on after them,
what is left of the humble and good life
in the trackless deserts
of human endeavor?
And what does it profit us
to be humble
if the proud thrive
at our expense?

By the world's standards
humility is anything but an asset.
Yet there is no pain too heavy to be borne
to earn this great prize.
Like the seed that bursts forth
to clothe the tree with blossoms
which then fruit with new seeds a hundredfold,
humility gives back again
a million times its own sweetness.

Contentment and humility
are brothers and sisters
of the spiritual path.

May you be born humble
so that you may learn the secret
from life's great teacher.

PRIDE

I was sitting in a bar
talking with my father
and wondering why I was born to him
and what could he teach me.
He had been drinking heavily
and friends had asked me to speak to him.
They said, "You are the only one
he will take any notice of."

I looked at him,
a man of some seventy years
and myself nearly fifty.
He looked back into my eyes
as I asked him,
"What is the cause of your drinking, Father?
You must have some disappointment
or insecurity about life;
what is really in your heart and mind?"

He looked at me and said,
"I am quite happy here
in the warm sunny Caribbean
and I am ready to die when my time is up."

I said to myself,
"What a lack of ambition,
what a useless life lived
to have no purpose but to sit and die."

I looked in his eyes
and saw that expression
I had seen since youth,
quizzical, faintly gentle,
and with a hint of steel blue determination.

*How could this be **my** father*
spending all his money on rum?

I decided to shame him into looking at his situation.
"What have you done, Father, in life,
which is important?
What have you got
to teach a son about life
and what have you learned from it?"

"My son," he said,
looking me straight in the eye
with a mixture of love and penetration,
*"You **are** my words and thoughts,*
and ever since you were born
you have said and done
all the things I have been thinking
but could never express."
Not satisfied with this answer,
however flattering,
I decided to test him further.

"Well, I know you are very
proud of me and all that I have achieved,
but what have you actually created
with your own life forces
that were given to you by God?"

He looked at me with eyes
both imploring and loving
with the blaze of passion
that I had only once seen before
when I was a small boy
asking him to protect me from a bully.
"My son, where were you when you were
but a thought in my mind?

What do you think I was doing
when your mother and I
conceived you in the depths of passion?
I have lived for nothing else
and no other purpose
but to bring you into this world.
That is my finest achievement,
and all that I have ever wanted to be
and all that I have thought of doing
has been done by you."

He looked at me with a penetrating gaze
that went to the depths of my soul
and I knew the humility of my own father.

I knew my own pride
and felt the judgements of my father
leave my heart
as he sat there looking at me
as manifestation of his own self.

"That is the only important thing
I ever did," he said.
"Is it not enough that you are sitting there
talking to me
and expressing all my own secret thoughts?"

I felt humiliated by my own pride of
achievement and was brought
to the knowledge of my humble beginnings.

For I had met a truly humble man
who had penetrated my most secret self
with his own humility.

BANANA LEAF

6

The teeming life of Mother Ganges is timeless.

We were walking beside the big river at Patna and the Ganges flowed by on its way from Benares to the ocean. Floating in the murky waters were bits of corpses from the burning funeral ghats and the excreta of a hundred and ten cities. I wondered, how can anyone have considered this water holy for so many centuries. As we walked we came across some peasants who were doing their morning spiritual ablutions by the riverside. They were being led by a devout Brahmin priest who was chanting Twam Eva Mata (Thou Art The True Mother). We passed them and in the distance we stopped and looked back.

Overlooking the scene before us with all its color and devotion, I began to think of the timeless centuries in which this scene had been enacted and viewed by others through the cycles of history. Kings and empires had fallen, great wars had been fought, and India had been plunged from the light of the worldwide Buddhist surge of devotion into the darkness of the Mogul conquerors. I was enthralled by a scene which had remained the same over two thousand years. I heard his voice speaking softly beside me.

"Oh Holy Mother Ganges," he said, "How they throw all the dirt and filth into your lifeblood and pollute your waters that come down from Rishikesh. Yet you are pure and are the life of the cities and all the peasant families and farmers along the way." I knew he was reading my thoughts when he said: "Life is like a holy river of consciousness, people are forever throwing their junk into its purity. Look how they abuse it and yet it still carries on."

I knew he was referring to the politicians in the government who were clamoring for us to start a research center for the study of kundalini energies and all of them were scrambling to get grant money like a lot of monkeys after nuts. He sighed and looked at the flowing water. We had just had the first meeting of the Institute of Psychic and Spiritual Research in Delhi and we had got a loan to build a center right next to the Holy Man's Serving Association. Although the association had 80,000 sadhus as members, the spiritual politics and backbiting among the gurus of India saddened him deeply. He looked at me and said, "Whatever they do to the pure river it will continue to give of its holy blessings. A life that is lived amongst the filthy Ganges waters can still be as pure as the spirit which purifies it."

I began to think of all the hassles of doing anything at the national level of life in India in 1961, and I knew he was referring to my own service for the Universal government which one day will govern the planet earth.

It was a timeless moment and a subtle lesson in constancy and persistence. The enormity of the task was daunting. The premonitions of the hurdles and obstructions to world renewal came flooding into consciousness like a negative cloud of unknowing. Only the thought that all was possible with God kept me in a state of faith. He sighed again and turned away from the timeless picture burning itself in the brain behind my eyes. He looked sad

We were on our way to meet the Prime Minister of Bihar State in another part of town. We walked along the river path a little. Suddenly he turned off into a rice field and followed a narrow pathway of feet-beaten earth. Soon we came to a peasant's hut at the edge of the rice field. He marched into the empty hut and sat down on the floor motioning me to sit against the thatched wall beside him.

I gave him a bewildered look as he said, "We will eat here." There was nothing to see except a fiber mat on the floor.

Presently a dark skinned coolie ran in the hut shouting Guruji, Guruji, at the top of his voice with a look of absolute joy on his face. He kissed the yogi's feet and ran out and got a banana leaf to spread on the floor. In a matter of minutes a pan of hot rice appeared which the peasant proceeded to dole out with his dirty fingers onto the banana leaf. I thought that's a funny kind of plate to eat off; why these people must be so poor they don't even have plates.

In his enthusiasm the coolie dropped a handful of rice on the floor between the pan and the yogi's banana leaf. It was a dirty floor and I thought what a pity for such a poor person to waste even a handful of rice. Before anyone could say anything the Guru picked up the rice out of the dust and popped it in his mouth. I reacted with all my western tradition of purity. He looked at me and chewed the rice very deliberately and then smiled.

I was completely shocked into the realization that my ideas of purity were totally different from his. The idyllic setting of temples and the holy Ganges river and scenes of devotion were all around me, but here in the midst of poverty, dirt and soil, the Guru brought back to me vividly the true root of the word humility, meaning of the soil—the humus. Here was I, a Romantic at heart, trying to be spiritually ruthless and scientific, when none of it was of any real meaning in the chewing of a handful of precious dirty rice in a peasant's tiny hut. Idyllic Ganges scenes of purity and washing the body did not mesh with the harsh realities of humble lives.

The Guru signalled me to attend to my dusty banana leaf with its little heap of rice and lentils on it. I stared at it and thought, how bizarre this whole trip is, to have this kind of breakfast on the way to see a Prime Minister. I got the distinct impression I was dreaming it. I was living in some bizarre waking dream, some bizarre cosmic movie theatre with real rivers, real coolies and a real Guru. When I ate the rice off the banana leaf with my fingers I knew it was real. It was the best rice I have ever tasted!

"He looked at me and then smiled."

HAPPINESS

Happiness is the thought of fullness and gratitude
for what we have already received from life.
How beautiful life is
when gratitude gives meaning
to the song of birds
and the breathing of the trees,
and thoughts of giving
become an expression of the One.
For in your heart is One who would give all
to know the ultimate Self giving
and receive the eternal bliss of contentment.

The blessing of the now is in the giving of gratitude
for the greatness of heart to be found all around us.
And worry of the future is mistrust of the benign One.

Even the smallest flower sings a hymn of goodness
to the morning sun.
To be well pleased with our gift of life
is the root of all humility
and the great secret of happiness.

"Whosoever shall exalt himself shall be abased; and he that shall humble himself shall be exalted." Matthew 23:12.

GRAVITY, LEVITY

We were walking down a pathway by the river and he gazed out over the water until I sensed him far away in some strange space. I wondered what spaces there were out there beyond all this human scene. Were there beings of great light? Were there masters of worlds within worlds within worlds? When would I know what made this universe spin and these atoms dance their circles in matter? The same force that made the river flow to its lowest levels in the oceans, made the earth stay in its gravitating orbit. I wondered why all the planets needed to hold together in one system. Was the nature of gravity a powerful attraction like my love for him? He began to speak from that strange space like a voice that was coming out from the water of the flowing river:

> *"When we flow with life*
> *lower and higher are ONE.*
> *When lower and higher are ONE*
> *gravity and levity*
> *become in and out.*
> *In and out*
> *becomes breathing.*
> *The whole universe*
> *breathes in with gravity*
> *and breathes out*
> *with levity and light."*

He looked at me very gravely and I went into myself Suddenly he smiled and was all light. I came out of my grave feelings and expanded into his joy. I had begun to breathe with the cosmos, and I knew I would never breathe an ordinary breath ever again.

A VISIT TO THE
PRIME MINISTER

On the banks of the river, all footprints are made in the same mud.

We were walking by the River Ganges in an outlying district of Patna. We had just had some rice and lentils cooked for us by a riverside peasant farmer and then we had resumed our way into town. The Guru had told me that day we were going to see the Prime Minister of Bihar state and I was anxious to enlist his support for the Insitute of Psychic and Spiritual Research that we were starting in New Delhi.

I was getting excited as we neared the great city of six million souls. I began to wonder how the Guru had made an appointment with such an important personage because I had been with him constantly hour by hour for over three weeks. There was just no way he could have made any contact. In my mind, I began to question his judgement. Were we going to walk all the way through the great suburbs of Patna to the Prime Minister's palace? Patna was a huge sprawling city, the capital of India's most populous state with more population than the whole of Great Britain. The streets went on for miles and I did not fancy walking through the slums of six million people until we got to the capital at the center. I began to get concerned because it was already eleven in the morning and I was sure we could not make the Prime Minister's office before he finished seeing people for the day unless we got a real move on.

The Guru seemed unconcerned with Time and nothing seemed to bother him. I was so used to the western habit of respecting everyone's time that I was still having trouble getting used to the way this Guru just walked into strange houses and plonked himself down without asking anybody.

We walked along the riverbank watching the ferry boats as we got into the outer streets of this great mass of mediocre houses. We turned off towards the center and were walking past a bazaar thronged with thousands of people jostling elbow to elbow among the traffic. My feet were getting tired of slogging the uneven roads. The Guru marched on.

Suddenly a loud honking of a horn sounds behind us. We turn round and there is a round-faced Indian with a very posh car leaning out of the window shouting "Guruji, Guruji, I have come to take you to my house to have some lunch." People seemed to crowd round and show interest and someone in the crowd made a passage for the Guru to get to the car doors.

"Come," the Guru said, "we will eat at his house."

I thought immediately that if we wasted time socializing now we would never get to the Prime Minister's office in time. We should ask the guy to drive us straight there instead.

"What about the Prime Minister?" I said dubiously.

He said, "Don't worry. We must first eat," and again I thought to myself, "He's got all his priorities the wrong way round. It should be business first, eat second."

We arrived at our friend's home and every luxury food was provided as our host seemed to be a wealthy Indian merchant in a very poor town. The meal was splendid and after the eating we were offered beds to rest on for an afternoon nap. The Guru curled up and was asleep in a moment and I was left wondering if all this talk of seeing the Prime Minister was all hot air and a lot of egotism. He was just trying to impress me with big talk.

It must have been about four o'clock in the afternoon when we got a message that a car had come for us. I went outside to the door and saw a great big long official-looking Rolls Royce with a governor's banner displayed on a little staff over the front hood. I was told this car used to belong to the Governor's Palace when the British ruled India and that now it was used by the Prime Minister on official business. The uniformed chauffeur jumped smartly out of the driving seat and saluted the Guru, so I figured he must be a soldier. He spoke smilingly to the Guru with obvious pleasure at being able to deliver his message:

"The Prime Minister sends his respects to the Swami and heard he was at this residence and requests that you come to the palace for dinner," he said with military precision while standing at full attention.

The Guru smiled at him and said, "You go back to your Prime Minister and tell him he has to come in person to invite me, not send a messenger."

I was shocked! What an insult to refuse a genuine offer of a man's table. What arrogance to put oneself up so high that one could not just humbly accept the Prime Minister's offer. Besides, here on our own doorstep was the transport ready and waiting. I was sure the Prime Minister's ego would not bother to humiliate itself and would invite someone else instead, someone more gracious, more appreciative, less egotistical. I felt ashamed. Yet at the same time I thought how strange that the Prime Minister only had to hear this Guru was in town to track him down, rather than us wonder how on earth we were going to get there. I realized this bizarre Guru had some strange power to turn everything upside down. Instead of going he was coming. Instead of asking he was telling, instead of bowing and scraping before important people, he told them to bow, but made the humble feel like kings. But this time I figured he had blown it. He had just gone too far, I thought, and would either get no reply, or the Prime Minister would just write him off as an arrogant egomaniac.

We sat on the front verandah talking with our host, who did not seem quite as shocked as I was but was obviously a little disturbed because a Prime Minister was a very important person to a businessman. I thought maybe he was the one who had telephoned the Prime Minister's office out of his own self-importance after hearing the Guru say he was on his way there. He looked definitely nervous and I knew he was feeling the same way as I was. We had blown it!

I was sitting looking out at the street traffic crowding past the front door, when I noticed a big car coming down the street. It had the same flag on it. Could it be that the Prime Minister had actually swallowed his pride and come personally? The car pulled up to the curb and the door was flung open and out rushed the Prime Minister, stumbling in his haste to get up the steps and pushing past me sitting in my chair, he hurled himself at the Guru's feet, fawning all over him and kissing his feet like an abject slave, enough to sicken me with his obvious servility. Something I could never do to any man!

"I am sorry Guruji, sorry I did not come personally. I know what you are trying to teach me. Man must come to God, not expect God to come to man."

I watched him profusely kissing the Guru's feet again and was profoundly shocked for the second time. Could such a politician and manipulator of votes and people be really humiliating himself kneeling in this abject fashion?

Then the Guru did another startling thing. He literally slapped the Prime Minister in the head and it looked like a good punch with all his strength. The Prime Minister fell back from the blow and I thought he was going to fall over, but he recovered his balance and I noticed a look of absolute bliss appear on his face.

"Oh Guruji, a hit from you is a divine blessing," he said and he stayed entranced for quite a few minutes, constantly repeating, "Thank you, Thank you, Thank you Guruji," in a refrain like a hymn.

I thought, "I cannot be experiencing this. It is just too bizarre. I must pinch myself to see if I am really here witnessing this whole embarrassing scene. No westerner would have taken this kind of nonsense. Hitting disciples is not the way of a holyman. Violence should not be necessary. Besides it's all so topsy-turvy and upside down. Gurus should be all light and humility, they should . . . etc.," and then I caught myself making judgements of 'shoulds' and 'oughts' and 'mights' and 'coulds' and looked up at the others crowded around me who had all witnessed the same thing. I was amazed with what I saw.

The Indian merchant was standing there with his eyes closed with exactly the same look of bliss on his face as the Prime Minister. I looked at the others and everyone all around had that certain smile and was completely silent and unselfconscious with the same bliss. They were vicariously sharing in the Prime Minister's breakthrough! This fellow had seen his own arrogance and was transformed into humility. He had invited the swami because of a selfish motive to decorate his palace with holy vibes and had been collecting swamis and gurus for their political value. He had seen through his egotism.

Gradually the Prime Minister's expression came back to normal but he had a radiant smile. The Guru looked at him in a very direct way and said, "Now we will come to your palace!"

We were going to dine with the Prime Minister after all, and what's more we would be on time; but it would not be for an appointment at the office. At the realization of how the events of the day had turned out and my misgivings of only an hour or two ago, the swiftness of events was almost too much for me. I was open-mouthed with awe! I thought to myself, "Only in India could this happen." It was just too incredible for anywhere else.

The dinner was excellent. We ate off the official state plates and posh western style gilt cutlery for me. We stayed the night at the Palace at the Prime Minister's invitation. That night I dreamt I was eating dinner off banana leaves on a dirty floor.

THE EFFORTLESS EFFORT

The pressures of life
are born out of resistance.
The effort that is made
is proportional to resistance felt.

Running fast is difficult
over difficult ground.
Running slow over easy ground
is no challenge but only good exercise.
Both challenge and exercise
come from doing what is difficult.

Can you learn to run slow with the many
and remain fast in the One?
Can you deal with great tasks
while they are still quite small?
Can you discover the resistance
before the effort is made?

Can you change in your soul
before the immobility of its shell cracks?

BECOMING WHOLE

The energy of the healer
is the energy of the universe
moving into wholeness.

Life is the healer
and life experience is the teacher.

Our dis-ease is our lesson from life.
Our wholeness is our blessing from life.

Wholeness is holiness.

The sun is whole because it is one vast
wave of light
and each planet is a pressure wall
in the whole standing wave.
The dimensions of this wave
resonate with the dimensions of our
own particular wave.
The psychic centers are wheels of energy
which mark the pressure walls
of vibrating systems of Being
in the whole universe.
Man functions in his mind and Being
as nature functions in the solar system;
the planets are but the chakras
of the sun.

The sun's light is a vast outward breath.
Its gravitational pull
is its inspirational breath.
Man is healed by breath,
and the wholistic breath
is a complete breath.

Light conquers gravitation
when the outward breath radiates
the surplus excitation of bliss
in order to stay whole.

To give light and radiate to the whole
is to receive holiness in return.

Be thou whole.
Be thou healed.
Be thou the beaming sun
and bathe your chakras with light.
Be thou immersed
in the breath of holiness.

A TEST OF FAITH

8

The Guru at the Temple of Vishnu with the Parliamentary Secretary of the Science Congress of India (left) and Dr. Vinekar, Director of a yogic hospital (right).

I was at a remote place in the heart of Bihar State
far away from the busy metropolis of Patna. At this place
in the middle of a desolate rocky area, someone many
centuries ago had built a temple around a special pool
which was said to have healing powers. The place was
visited by pilgrims from all over India who walked long
distances to be able to sit in its holy waters. The pool was
called the Pool of Vishnu and there was a section for males
and another for females which were separated so that all
the pilgrims could undress in the open and go into the
pool without any clothes on. Right where the people took off
their clothes there was a spigot of a hot spring fountain of
water under which we were expected to wash the dust and
dirt off from our bodies before going into the holy waters
of the pool.

I was a bit nervous because this temple was reserved for
Hindus only and was regarded as a very holy place where
foreign visitors and tourists were forbidden to enter.
My skin was browned by the sun almost black, and my
robes of a sadhu and a sanyassin protected me from
suspicion. I was also with a great yogi who regarded me as
his son, but I knew that when I undressed, parts of my body
would be so white that someone would recognize that I
was a European and possibly cause a religious problem,
since there were just as many Indian fanatics in the religious
sense as there are in the West. I undressed rather hesitatingly
in the bright sun with the old man who threw off his garb
and rushed down a dark narrow steep stone passage of
steps to the pool which I could not see from the washing
place.

I walked to the head of the rock steps and looked down at
the Pool of Vishnu only to be greeted by a situation of
horror. There was my yogi getting in the dark dirty waters
of the pool up to his neck surrounded by the pressing

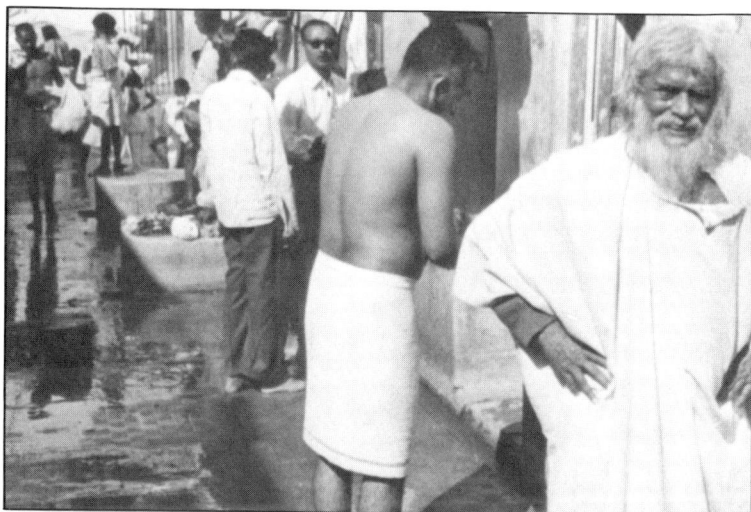

Just prior to going into the healing pool.

The Temple of Vishnu is magnificent. The pool in which men are healed is a crude stone pit in the ground inside the Temple.

bodies of all India's sick and diseased. Contagious disease and leprosy, people with oozing sores and swollen eyes, open wounds and bodies twisted by venereal disease and all the direst horror of the plagues of man seemed to be concentrated skin to skin in that tightly packed pit. I hung back in terror while the yogi beckoned me to come, showing me it was harmless by ducking his white flowing head under the surface of the filthy waters.

"Come, come," he shouted. "It will purify you!" All my training said that disease would be transmitted through millions of microbes infesting the waters.

"Come, come," he shouted again, "Holy water," pointing down at the water.

I had a horrible vision of dying in India from leprosy or some incurable disease. I had not built up any immunity like these Indian natives. The vision gave me one of the reasons why Europeans were forbidden to visit this temple. I looked down at the vision of the dimly lit pit and covered my eyes at the sight. Was it some mad dream I was having or was I being asked to enter this fearsome pit of Hell as some bizarre test? I thought of all my training in spiritual healing. I looked back at all my successes with the sick and the power of magic. Was this for real or was my good sense telling me to stay out of this dirty hole?

The Swami beckoned me again to come in close beside him, pushing one of the lepers to the side to make a space for me. My instinct was to turn back and put my clothes on. But another voice inside me said, "How come your mind and spirit are afraid for the body? How come you preach the power of yoga and spiritual powers to others and yet you shrink from a few bacteria?" I knew I had to do it or never look myself in the face again. "Go into the infested water and prove the power of mind over matter," another inner voice said. "How can you teach the Supreme power of the Spirit over matter and then not apply it?"

I started slowly down the steps and lowered myself reluctantly into the water in that dim pool, squeezed between the yogi who was encouraging me and a man with horrible sores around his neck. I gazed transfixed by those open sores now about ten inches from my own body while the Swami kept dipping his head in the water as if to say, "see it's alright, it's holy." I filled myself with white light and called down the host of heaven and the Christ light too. I was well in the water now and looking at the statue of Vishnu which the pilgrims were touching and splashing with water. I touched the statue too, for extra protection, for after all I was healthy and these people, except for the yogi, were all deathly sick. I remember checking my whole body mentally for scrapes or scratches in my skin where germs could get in. Then I thought of the natural openings of the anus and genitals and instinctively tightened them while praying more fervently that the water was indeed holy and pure. The yogi asked me to put my mouth, eyes, ears and head under water but I could not go deeper than my chin.

Soon the yogi got out and went up the steps to the world of light above. I quickly followed him feeling purified of fear but grateful to be away from the smell of sick bodies. I had conquered something in myself. Somehow I had a new radiant faith in myself and I knew I would not catch any of the diseases I had seen in the pool. A vibrant field of force was swirling in and around me like a pool of electricity.

I felt clean and white as snow in the being as well as the body. The whole world seemed like new, because I was new. I had discovered my real body, the indestructable, immortal body, made of Supreme Consciousness by the creator

101

Himself. I knew that our bodies were made of that swirling and vibrant stuff of creation that was in and around me now. My cells tingled. Even now, years later, they are still tingling from this experience and they have never stopped knowing the power of God and the heavenly host.

May this unnameable power be sensed
in the center of all your cells.

May this ONE be present in all your
eyes and openings.

May the ONE be vibrating in all your hearts.

May you BE the ONE in all eyes and
all hearts, and know the presence of Christ
as you pierce the memory of birth and rebirth.

May you know the power of God
and discover your immortal body.

May your body become one with the ONE.

WHAT IS LOVE?

Secret and mysterious is love,
a Holy Communion of ecstatic concentration
that calls eternally
towards cosmic consciousness.
Love is your progenitor
and the flower which fruits
in the secret garden of the heart.

Melting the madness of the mind,
love can also smelt the metallic hardness
of a mighty pride.
Love churns the heart,
softens the strong as butter,
excites the dull,
and terrifies the timid.
Yet it was love that set
you forth in your mother's womb
and it was love that glinted
in your father's eye
and was worth the effort.

Love moves you quickly
into a slavery to your genes
and inches you slowly
towards your cosmic lover.
In and out is the divine motion.
All lovers know
the climax of emotion
when, sweetly flowing
like drops of bliss
falling upon the ocean,
we become as ONE.
Hallowed be the name
of that Supreme Love.

BEAUTY

It was said of old,
"Beauty is Truth,
Truth Beauty.
That is all ye know on earth
and all ye need to know."

But what of the feeling heart?
Is not beauty more than
words and aphorisms?

The poets sing,
"A thing of beauty is a joy forever.
Its loveliness increases;
it will never pass into nothingness."

And what is nothingness
to a heart that is already
empty of love?

Fine words are sometimes just the surface
of those whose hunger for love
may never be met.
If the love they yearn for
does not come
and the beauty of their devotion
does not flower,
then the disappointment
of one who lost heart in life
will stand as reality
behind the beauty of the words.

Poets may sing of Truth
but my song says
beauty is not always Truth
and Truth is often ugly.

A thing of beauty can pass away,
its loveliness transcended
by the joy of nothingness.

Who can feel the power of nothing
until something is taken away?
Rich become bankrupt
lovers become bereft
thrill becomes misery
life becomes death.

In nothing there is everything
both ugly and beautiful
and what is beauty rests
on what is ugly.
What is seen is conditioned
by our consciousness.

Attachment to beauty
as an eternal joy
may bring feasting
and exaltation of the lewd.
For doth not the glutton see beauty
in the sensual goodness of his food?
And does not lust see beauty
as a reflection of its
own insatiable appetite?

I have seen
the beauty of pure consciousness
in an ugly form;
I have seen the radiance of beauty
in the blazing light of Lucifer.
In the smooth curves of beauty
can lie the downfall of great men,
the betrayal of all Truth.

Though you may sing of beauty,
of Truth and goodness as eternal,
yet I have seen goodness
taken to a fault.
What is important
is to see the helplessness of deep love,
the humiliation of desire,
the fear of our great loss.
For in the conquering and absence
of these, there is great beauty everywhere.
There is Truth as ruthless and sharp
as a surgeon's knife.
There is beauty as jagged
as lightning.

For He who created all above
loves all below,
both ugliness and beauty equally.
That love which sees
beauty and goodness in all things
knows that all things
pass eternally into nothingness
and are reborn as Truth
in every form of life.

You are beauty and Truth
and goodness
and you are all the ugliness too.

My song is saying
beauty is not always Truth
and Truth is often ugly.
What is beautiful may not be Truthful
and fine words may not be true words.
Look beneath beauty
to find what is above.
Look not to beauty but to love.

FOR THE SAKE
OF BEAUTY

9

All that is beautiful will one day become dust, but spirit is eternal.

We were just coming out of a temple on the bank of a wide river and I felt as though something had happened to me in my meditations. It was as if some spirit had pulled me upwards out of the flesh and cleaned me out and I was all new. The Guru was walking by my side. As we came out of the dim interior into a shaft of sunlight I felt all clean and new, and a pure feeling of excitement was bubbling inside me. Everything I looked at seemed to have this quality of freshness. Even the material world was a feast of colors and a vibrant answering signal to the intensity of internal stimulation.

Suddenly it happened. As we reached the brow of a small hill on the pathway to the river we came upon two golden brown sculptured girls holding their long saris out in the breeze after washing them in the river. They were standing modestly behind these delicate silk cloths with the sun shining through. What they did not know was that the sun's light made the silk completely transparent and the beautiful shapes of their bodies and breasts were silhouetted sharply against the gossamer thin fabric. I was shocked by the impact of so much beauty and instantly caught the vision of the voluptuous temple carvings of the ancient Indian sculptors who had delighted in the very essence of the female form. What a timeless moment, I thought, as I stood for a second drinking in the brilliance of the rare scene. I feasted my eyes on the beauty of it all and stood like a god-artist viewing the canvas of his own creation. The Guru stopped also and turned to me and caught my vibration.

"Stop that!" he said, giving me a backhanded clout across the wrist which I can still feel to this day.

"Stop what?" I said, turning to him in consternation.

"Cut that out," he said sternly, and I was shocked and felt misunderstood.

Protesting that I was almost seeing a vision of God in the beauty before my gaze, it occurred to me he might have a hang-up about women. I thought that anyone who could misread the beautiful thoughts I was having and mistake them for sexual lust after bottoms and busts was really screwed up in his bottom chakra. After all, sex in India was obviously a major occupation, since they had an over-population problem. I knew that yogis who preached abstinence often had sex with their disciples. So I immediately judged the Guru. In my culture you could see sensual pictures in every Playboy magazine, but this scene was different, like a pure spiritual experience of Beauty. It was obvious that he didn't buy it. I looked at him and saw a look of disapproval which I seldom saw, and I couldn't get in touch with whatever it was he was seeing.

It took me several years pondering about this weird incident to understand what was behind his action. Was I as pure in my looking as I thought? I was hung up on beauty and whenever I saw it in paintings, in the sleek lines of an animal or in the golden light of the sunset, I could feast on it like most people drooled over a fabulous meal. Beauty of shape and color and form and light and all that gave the aesthetic thrill was deeply ingrained in my hunger. Hairs stood up on my neck when I saw a good painting or a sculpture by Rodin. Beauty was a shot of vitamins! I was attached to beauty and savored it hungrily like a salivating dog looking for its bone, but I had not been able to see my attachment to it. The wise yogi had seen that attachment and I had not.

Remorse set in. So many years had passed before my realization that attachment to anything, however beautiful, was an enslaving of the mind and a binding of the heart.

I had thought that beauty, like Truth, could be worshipped—
was one of the eternal truths itself—and that one could
legitimately feast upon it and call it holy. Like Keats, I
felt that such vision was "all ye know on earth and all ye
need to know." I examined all the lusts for life I had seen in
others and myself. The side to side motion of certain girls'
bottoms and the velvet smoothness of God-created flesh.
If it was not appreciation of beauty, what was it? I thought
of King David and his lust for Bathsheba. I entered into
him and saw through his eyes. Would I, like David, send
my general to his death for the sake of beauty, though
the wisest Solomon be my son born of the urge? I found
in myself compassion for David who wore sackcloth and
ashes for his sin: I found love for God for giving me the
passion; I found love for Christ, born in the line of David,
for making the passion of his forebear's loins into love
of the One.

THE TUNNEL OF LOVE

The tunnel of love is fraught
with subtle traps of selfishness,
and impure thoughts are caught
which lead us to the school
where selfless love is taught.

Lovers beware of that dark tunnel
whose entrance is bathed
in blazing light,
for love is not always playful
with devotees of light.

Love does not wander
or fall asleep with a dull mind.
Love is always aware of what is loved.
Love knows its intentions
and is full of attention
but is blind to all risks.
Love is therefore dangerous.

The path of love
is not a tunnel for timid souls,
but to reach the cave of love
the strong and fearless
must be soft as a lily,
sweet as ambrosia,
passionate with understanding,
for those who hurt the tenderness of love
will themselves be shot by love's arrow,
cut by the sharp pain of her surgeon's knife,
sliced in two by the longing of separation.

The tunnel of love
is long and endless
until the lover stops and listens.

True love is the first whisper
of the gentle inner throb
at the subtle center
of the Supreme Self,
ceaselessly seeking
to set love free
from its separate cave.

Love illuminates the eye
and expands the aura
until the heart is sure,
for love never stops flowing
until our consciousness is pure.

The universe and everything in it
is an outward flow of love.
It is the song of love
whose creation is a crystallized form
of unceasing upwelling joy.

Love is made pure
more by pain than bliss.
Yet like childbirth,
the joy of birthing washes away
all memory of pain.
Thus one great lover
did inspire the world
to forget its pains
in a blazing passion play of love.
Love comes crowned with thorns
before lifting us up
into the joyful light of Heaven.

DESIRE AND LOVE

Nothing exists without a desire to BE.
From atom to man
all things live in a Kingdom of Desire.

Ultimately desire is the cause of all matter.
All people continue their existence
through their desire of form.
Desire is with all of us from before the beginning,
but it is love which takes life along its path.
Thou art that love flowing into life,
thou art the silent love
which has no voice to speak,
thou art the glory of love
which sings at the cradle of a child.

Desire dominates all our thoughts
and rages at the root of all suffering.
Desire separates in sexual sensations,
creating yearning for the other.
All Desire is written in the juices of creation
as it is written in the human blood.

All motion and vibration come out of the center of this Desire.
Two opposite forces,
male and female, positive and negative,
make up the evolutionary Desire for stillness in all things.
Sex desire is at the heart of every atom
and blazes at the fiery heart of every star.
Light shines through space as the continuous
cosmic orgasm at the center of all Desire.
Sex balances all systems through desire.
Desire of the other Self is sexually polarized
between the unity of two and the oneness of all.

Desire is not quenched until the two forces
of surrender and projectivity are equal.
Therefore when ONE is found, Desire becomes love.

Love is the blessing of the Divine
the mighty spark of Father Time
quenched by Mother Force
dawning in the human heart.
Blazing in the divine dawn of life,
your divinity is the fullness of love.
Be alive to love.
Keep your heart sensitive to love.
Do not disturb the bliss of love
with the worldly noises of separation,
for love is your teacher
and is the author of all that is divine.
Life's goal is the abundance of the loving heart.

The waves of love
ripple through our lives
to awaken our soul to its source.
The desire for God and Brahman
is not the true love of the One
because this love of God
is a by-product of desire.
In union with God we cannot love something other.

The branching tips of the universe
reach into limitless space
infinitely expanding its author's desire.
And the same divine Light
reaches inward to all hearts.
Choking the voice with blissful emotion
the divine Self swells up the heart into the mouth
and love manifests in all its unspeakable power.

In union there is no other
only the love of the One,
the ultimate singularity.

The One I love
is strong and tender
but being shy
hides in the heart.

CAN YOU SEE YOUR TRUE SELF?

Higher than the highest spirit
and lower than absolute nothing,
the Supreme Self
sits at the centerless center
in the heart of all existence,
viewing itself in all beings.

Can I tell you this
or must you catch it
in the subtle worlds
of direct perception?
Can you see your true Self
without going far beyond the senses?
Can you see the Christ within,
without going beyond the mind
and even beyond the beyond?

Until you have loved the One
absolutely,
without limits,
totally as your self,
God is but a concept
and you cannot see
or know
what you do not know.

THE
COSMIC BABY

10

First meeting with my grandaughter.

It was a festival day in Ranchi, a town with a temple which attracted many pilgrims from outlying districts. We had been meditating in the Shrine to Vishnu and the Guru had chanted the OM at the top of his voice on several octaves. I had felt, "Why is he making such a song and dance about it?" To suddenly burst out in the middle of the quiet meditation with a loud OM seemed to be an effort to attract attention to oneself. I began to doubt his motives. He was just like a large, immature child making a noise in the temple when everyone else was peaceful and quiet. I felt embarrassed. Why couldn't he just meditate quietly like me and all the other ordinary, humble people instead of going through this routine with the chanting? He hadn't asked anyone if they wanted to hear the chanting of OM but had assumed that all present needed to hear. For some reason I felt at that time that he was being childish and blind to his own effect on people. I began to doubt whether he had any insight at all into the nature of Being. He could not see himself as he really was, doing all these antics. Whatever would all these people think?

We were walking down the pathway out of the temple when we reached a spot outside where we could sit and watch the people come and leave on their way to and from worship. On the way out of the temple I had noticed this very attractive young woman with a small child in her arms meditating. The child had seemed particularly peaceful and I remembered thinking what a picture of mother and child she would have made for the Italian master painters of madonnas.

About ten minutes later I saw her walking down the path towards us with the child again, making her way over to the guru. She began to thank him for chanting the OM and was saying how whenever she heard him chant, everything became so peaceful in her life, how the child had heard it and then settled down. I began to think I had misjudged him and his bursting out in the silence of the temple. Maybe he had known there was someone in the temple who was disturbed?

I looked at the small child who was hardly more than three or four months old. In my imagination it had arms and legs of India rubber and moved them so cutely with its tiny fingers clasping and unclasping. I noticed how pure the baby was and could not resist bending over it and smelling the aroma of its skin. The young woman seemed particularly pleased at my interest in the child. Strange, I thought, Indian babies had that same baby smell that my own children had which I once thought was talcum powder smell. But I had found out since that all babies had this peculiar aromatic skin which suggested some special vibration or aura which disappeared when they grew older than three or four months.

I began to ponder this and looked deep into the clear eyes of the baby, held so tightly in his mother's arms. It seemed such a tiny thing, but what secret powers they had to captivate. I looked at the mother and asked would she mind if I played with its tiny fingers. She pushed the baby towards me. Its hand closed around one of my fingers. Out of the corner of my eyes I noticed the Guru had moved away and was standing about twenty-five feet away watching me. I decided the baby was so cute and such a lovely bundle of flesh in its uncontaminated, pure state, that I would try to make contact with it in depth. In the back of my mind I wondered if the Guru was leaving and was waiting for me.

There did not seem to be any urgency, so I put all my attention on the baby. I looked into the pure pools of its unwavering eyes. Strange, I thought, whenever I looked people straight in the eye they nearly always looked away

as if I was penetrating them, but this baby just looked me
back all the way like it had no self-consciousness at all.
I began to twiddle its fingers and make baby talk conver-
sation which went something like this:

Boo hoo little baby you.
What tiny little finger-dingers
you got stuck on your teeny-weenies.
Bubble and chuckle your chin and cheek
and tweek your little top knot
What a nice dandle
for daddy to handle,
to pat you on the botty
with your nosee wosy
a little snotty,
and a twiddling of your toesy.

With my free hand I tickled its "tosey wosies" as it
grabbed my other finger and put it in its toothless mouth.
I was just going to go into another delirious communication
in baby language when I heard the Guru shout:

"Come here quickly!" I resented being ordered around
just as I was playing with the baby and I resisted going
over there to see what he wanted. "Come quickly!" he said,
"I want to show you something."

"What is it?" I said, a bit annoyed that he had interrupted
the communication with the wide-eyed baby just as we were
getting some response.

"Never mind, just come here. I want to introduce you
to some one." There was no one standing with him. "Come
over here quickly," he said rather urgently.

I walked over the distance of twenty-five feet between
us rather impatiently, and he pointed back at the woman
with the baby. "You see that fellow standing there talking?"
he said. I looked. There was no one with the woman with the

baby. He said, "Look again. Don't you see someone talking with that baby?" I looked again, but this time I gathered he was referring to me and that I should imagine myself still talking to it. "Don't you see how that fellow is talking quite differently to that baby than to anyone else he has ever seen?" he said mysteriously. I looked back again, still no one with the baby, but I could gather he was referring to me.

"Now," he said, "get back inside that fellow and feel what it is like to be talking to a baby again, try to feel how you were inside yourself. What were you thinking, because I saw your real self standing there for the first time since you came on this trip with me?" I tried to get in touch with how I was feeling only a few moments ago. How had I been feeling? I got back inside myself.

He said, "You remember how you talked to that baby? Try to talk to me the same way!" It seemed foolish to talk to a grown man the same way as I had talked to the baby. "Get back inside yourself again and get the feeling the baby gave you." I went within and imagined how I would talk and be with it.

He said very quietly, "The baby did not threaten you, eh?" I nodded. "The baby is harmless with no strength to answer you back, eh?"

"That's right," I said.

"Well how do you feel when you are not talking to an ego, when you know the baby will not judge you?" I saw very clearly that I became egoless myself and unself-conscious. Although I felt a bit silly watching myself talk to the baby in the imagination, I was contacting a rare part of myself which I rarely showed to grownups.

"That person standing there is your real Self. I have been watching it for some time, but it disappeared when you came over here. Why don't you try talking with that Being to everyone? I am waiting like a baby for you to talk to me without you becoming defensive, without your image of yourself building up again, without feeling that you are talking to anyone who will judge you."

I was stunned. Never had I thought of myself as being defensive or as an ego constantly watchful of my personal identity. But I enjoyed that state when talking to babies; it felt good and clean and pure. The guru looked at me and smiled. "Go back to your real Self and play with the baby. Get in touch with me as the baby and you will one day relate to everyone the same, without ego, without the self-sense continually conditioning your actions and feelings."

I looked at him and my heart lifted. Could I really trust him not to think me silly if I talked to him in baby language? I was not yet ready to go that far with any adult. I went back to the baby and began to play with it again. I felt the inner space which he was seeing. He had loaned me his eyes to see with and feel my real self with. It would be hard to continually remember myself as talking to others like babies. I realized that I had been born again as a cosmic baby. In order to do as he said I had to become a baby myself. I had to get rid of that imposter who enters into me whenever a second person enters the room or approaches me.

How difficult, I thought, to be aware without any image of self, like a baby. Yet I had been one myself some long time ago in memory and was therefore an expert. How we forget our true selves and show to others only the image we have acquired through the knocks and efforts of a lifetime. I entered into my new baby self with some sheepish humility.

It was new and strange but liberating. The weight of the albatross was off my neck and that monkey the ego was off my back.

That monkey was to return again and again, but gradually I learned to remember whenever I thought of that temple and the experience of psychic nakedness. I had become open to my real silly self and for awhile did not care who saw the cosmic child within me. I wondered how he had put up with the other one so long. He must be a great lover, I thought.

My heart lifts now whenever I hear anyone call, "Come quickly, I have something to show you!" Maybe I can become a baby and look at myself again in a new way everyday. I shall never forget that discovery of my real Self.

YOU ARE LOVE

Know that you are love—
not just the love of persons
but the binding force of consciousness
that holds all things together
by the sheer power of loving,
and that there is nothing
in the universe
that is not so loved.
The heart cannot say
"Shall I love this much?"
or set limits on love.
It cannot help but love,
for the very light of consciousness
that pours from your eyes
upon all the created world
is love.
Even the one who says "I" in you
is love.

You are the living ground
of angelic realms
and the rising sound of glory
ringing out across the heavens.
You are made for love's enjoyment
and out of love you came into your flesh.
You are love's creation
and by love you will be ultimately consumed.
There is no escape from love
for life is love
and love is the power that will slay you,
conquer you, play with you,
and make you aware of who you are.

THE LOVE BEYOND ALL UNDERSTANDING

And what of real love?
Does it vary with each thinker
or is it beyond thought?

If Divine love be beyond the mind,
beyond the imagination,
if it passes all understanding,
how can we experience its splendor?

As the beaming sun shines
throughout the whole of space,
so do vibrations of real love
fill the whole heart.
First make the heart empty like space
and love will fill you wholly
and will brim over
and spill out
and inexhaustibly waste itself;
for your cup runneth over
when your love is full.

All who have loved with this fullness
have more than enough.
Humbly they kneel together
before the altar of love,
for love is Holy.
We cannot betray it
and still be made whole.
Only trust can bring complete love.

How can we understand love?
For when we fall in love we lose our reason.
To understand love go beyond
human understanding.

True love lives in eternal time
and only springs forth
in the sacred space of the heart.

Whatever the head says
the heart cannot stop its loving.
The head warns us uselessly,
We know what we should do,
we know what we ought to do,
we know what we want to do,
but the heart says, "I'm going into this thing,
even if it kills me."
The heart will not talk with the head again
until the scar tissue is thick
with silent pain.

Love and reason co-exist
only in those who learn
to reason by the heart.
Make the heart of love
into a gift for the ONE.
Understanding will come later.

THE GURU'S SON 11

"My son is also my Guru."

I had been away sitting by the banks of the Ganges at Benares and drinking in the timeless air of a thousand years, but I was back now in Calcutta to go with the Guru to attend a very important conference of India's highest yogis. The meeting was to be on science and spirituality and had been summoned by the first president of India, Rajendra Prasad. The conference was to take place at an ashram near Patna where the president had retired with some sickness.

I went into the building where the Guru lived in Calcutta. He always stayed there when he was not travelling in Delhi or elsewhere. I found him seated on a thin grass mat meditating. I sat down and joined him without saying anything and closed my eyes. The concrete floor began to get very hard without any cushion or pillows to sit on. I looked around the room again—absolutely nothing of comfort. I was just thinking how this Guru does not seem to care about aching bones or anything physical, when I heard his voice speaking to me.

He said to me: "I would like to know whether I should really go with you to this conference. So if you don't mind I will ask my son if I should go."

"What do you mean, ask your son?" I said, rather puzzled that a great guru needed to ask anybody but even more puzzled about his son.

He said, "Well you see my son is also my guru."

I was intrigued. This was a guru who had disciples who were gurus with millions of disciples and yet he was saying he had to ask his son. Then again I remembered he was always saying he had only one disciple—Himself. He was now saying he himself had a guru, yet I had known him almost a year and he never told me he even had a son, so

128

I was mystified. "Himself" of course meant you and everyone else in his way of talking. Maybe he meant "my son" in the same way that he called *me* his son. He was a very mystical person. He was full of double and treble meanings.

I asked him, "What do you mean by *your son*? You call everybody your son."

"No," he said, "I mean my son."

"Your real son?" I asked.

"Yes. My real son," he replied.

"You have a son?" I asked.

"Yes, you will meet my son tomorrow; it is time to sleep now."

"Where shall I sleep?" I asked.

He said, "Right where you are now."

I looked at the thin mat, with my bones already digging into the cold concrete. It was another test; if he could do it, so could I. So we slept side by side on the flat cold concrete. My mind was going round in circles. How come he had never said he had a real son?

In the morning we meditated and just before breakfast he suddenly announced, "Come along, I'll show you my son." He took me down a long dark narrow passage at the back of the house. He carried a small candle light for the two of us as we marched single file so it was difficult for me to see. It was strange that I did not know this passage existed and I began to think, as if in a dream-like state, that it must be a secret passage into the Mother Kali temple where I had heard all sorts of blood sacrifices went on to assuage her appetite for destruction.

The imaginings were quickly dispelled as we stopped suddenly. There at the end of the passage was a green door with three large bolts across it. Fastened on them securely hanging, like great hearts, were three huge padlocks. He reached deliberately into his robes and pulled out a great key as big as my hand. Dramatically he started to unlock these padlocks which must have measured six inches across and weighed a few pounds each.

This seemed really weird as everything was oversized. So I had to ask myself if I was having a dream. I thought, "No, it's real. I am really here and these are real locks and this is a real guru throwing open this door."

As he threw open the door he barked some command in a strange language into the dark space inside. What a funny place, I thought, whatever could be in there? In the half light I saw a very hairy creature scramble across the floor and try to climb up the wall. Why, he looks like a hairy spider, I thought.

The Guru shouted again into the black depths, and the creature came and sat in the doorway. It was a man! It was looking all over the universe at everything around it, shaking its head like some mongol child but never looking at me. His eyes were going in every direction except mine. Can this really be happening? I thought.

The Guru then turned to me and said rather sweetly, "This is my son. He has developed his heart at the expense of his head." I thought I must be dreaming, because this humanoid creature was covered in hair like some strange abominable snowman.

The Guru said, "I have to keep him behind these locks and bars because people cannot understand. But I use him only on occasions like this when I want to know something

130

about you. The only problem with my son is that he can only look at Truth. So, if you are not True in your heart, he will not look at you."

Here was this creature looking all over the universe except at me and I thought, "My God, you have to look at me! You have got to see the Truth in me."

The creature continued to look all over and I thought he was not going to look at me at all, so I started to examine myself. What had I done wrong in my life that he could not look at the Truth in me? I remembered that I had chased a cow with a sharp spike once when I was six years old and had felt very guilty at the time, and once I had put a fire-work into one of the brass bottles in the church and someone told the choir master. One by one I went through all my sins and they didn't seem so bad, but still he wasn't looking at me. Then I thought, "Well there is nothing wrong with me, I feel okay, I've no guilt in me." And at that moment he looked straight in my eyes and looked right in my soul and I've never seen eyes quite like that. They went straight through me and held my gaze for a few minutes and penetrated me through and through. They had the quality of the cow that I had chased plus the love in the eyes of a dog and the full gamut of human emotions all in one.

The Guru looked at me with compassion and said, "That's what I use my son for; he is my guru because his eyes can only see purity."

He meant of course that this strange creature in his heart was even more advanced than he was. It was difficult to believe my ears or my eyes. Here was a great guru saying his guru was a deformed lunatic. What was behind this strange dreamlike incident? While I was still wondering if it was all real, the Guru barked out another command and the creature scuttled back across the floor inside and tried to climb up the wall again. It had no mind, no human sense at all.

The Guru turned to me as I took a last look at a sight I never expected to ever see again in life. He said in a slow deliberate voice as if to let it sink in deeply, "I am sorry, but my son has developed his heart at the expense of his head." And with that he clanged the doors shut and placed the three huge padlocks on the three big bars across the door and marched back down the passage as if nothing had happened.

It left a very profound impression on me. To go through this experience after being with the Guru for a year was like taking part in some bizarre dream sequence. I never knew he had a son and to this day I still don't know whether this creature was a real son. It was a well kept secret. And if I asked him if it was his real son he would say yes because to him everyone was his real son in that sense. He was in a cosmic state of consciousness, so nothing was separate from himself. He called me his son but I wanted to know if the creature was his blood son or his spiritual son. "Yes, my son," he would say, looking up at the sun, meaning that all is one and that it cannot be separated in pure consciousness. In pure consciousness there is nothing there to separate itself.

I wondered how the creature was fed daily and remembered seeing a small trap door in one of the doors with a plate at the side. Food was put in by the household but no one was allowed to undo the locks at the end of that incredible long passage.

So we went to the conference, but ever since that experience in Calcutta I never knew what to expect next from this incredible holyman. Every day there was some lesson. I will always remember Calcutta and the deep brown eyes radiating with the light of pure consciousness. Many times I have seen them since, staring at me from the eyes of lovers and certain animals.

COMPASSION

In the burning flames of real love
in the hidden fires of compassion,
the heart which seeks
this spiritual beauty
shines with the radiance
of inner peace;
for real love is the dynamic process
of surrender to God,
the surrender of ego
to the egoless,
to the passion and inner compassion
of undeserved peace.

When the soul is feeling the lowest
and least deserving,
love sees the real self
and becomes compassion,
stupid and illogical,
caring and ruthless at the same time.

Compassion is undeserved love
given out of grace.

You can see compassion best
when it is not there.
When compassion is there,
you recognize it
by your own deep feeling of gratitude.
Man does not deserve
the compassion of God,
but God in His wisdom
is full of mercy.

Thus the world goes on in error and evil.
It exists solely
because of God's mercy.
But where there is no gratitude
there can be no mercy.
There is only love
waiting for an opening.

Compassion is the open heart
bleeding the ego to death
until the ocean of blood overflows
and becomes a caring current of love.

We learn to love ourselves
in the hidden fires of compassion.

Just as we are met with the same judgements
that we mete to others,
so too, when our heart
opens toward another,
love comes rushing back in
through the same opening.
He who learns this law of love
will dwell in the house
of his own compassion
and whomever he entertains
in that place
will feel that he has been
with God.

Compassion is not feeling sorry or sad
but the experience of warmth.
Compassion is a clear mind
uncluttered by achievements.

Compassion seeks nothing for itself.
Its spiritual beauty shines not for advantage
nor recognition from the One.
Compassion is joy and generosity of spirit,
the environmental radiation of Self
relating with people who cannot
drain our patience
because the supply is inexhaustible.

Can you imagine a compassion
like a burning flame of love
shining with the heat and passion
of a million suns?

Real love is a dynamic compassionate
surrender
to the inner passion of peace.

The love of anything but the One
is all a vanity of self.
The love of any separate one thing
is a separation from the One.
Compassion is oneness.
The strength of true love
when the heart is surrendered—
that is compassion.

IN SEARCH OF GRACE 12

Through self-sacrifice the self can know God.

There were parts of my personality that the Guru knew were defective. The ways he used to get beneath my ego were very strange and it took me many years to understand their full importance. Since I had spent several years in deep study I had a big investment in my own knowledge. It was very difficult to tell me anything; plus I was very sensitive to the slightest show of spiritual egotism because my own ego had done great battles with the need to be selfless. Inwardly I had some specific ideas about my own importance since some Indian horoscopes written by an ancient sage in the Brighu Samita had predicted my work and destiny which confirmed what I already had divined through meditation. But my head was larger than my heart and the Guru knew it. He would, like anyone else, have a tough problem getting me to be a disciple if there was even one flaw in his personality.

I was coming from a background of mysticism and meditation and had forced myself to learn many things in order to manifest what I came to do in this incarnation. I had made a study of psychic phenomena second to none and owned every book which had ever been published on the subject. I read much of the research written on this subject with very critical eyes since I could plainly see the mental gaps of experimenters and those interested in chasing reality through mediumship. I had studied physics avidly for explanations for the occult energies I had been privately researching and had developed powers of mind through the study of magic and healing through esoteric contact with those in the spiritual field, as well as methods of contacting Beings of light for the stepping down of cosmic forces. But I knew all this was not where it was at. There was a missing essence.

I was having to get more disciplined and scientific in order to express the spiritual realms in more concrete terms, more earthly energies. Coming from the mystic to the

material I was aware that I was going in the opposite
direction to most people who were striving to find masters
and gurus who would take them from the earthly plane
into the stratosphere of spiritual experiences. Hence
I had just as many conflicts in my contact with holymen
and people who had set themselves up as spiritual
authorities as I had with hard-nosed scientists who refused
to hear anything about psychic and spiritual energies.

I was the cosmic doubter who doubted even the doubters.
I was the doubter who knew that I was the doubter and the
doubt. Yet there was this problem in my personality of
surrender to someone who I did not feel knew even a
quarter of what I myself had forgotten. I had programmed
myself with so much information like an engorged
computer that it became difficult for me to remember
anything and to learn anything new. I desperately wanted
to meet someone to whom I could acknowledge my
ignorance in some form of humility and get some grace.
I was obsessed for two years with this idea of grace and
I knew all the doctrines of grace and the books about
grace and how humility could be feigned in the name
of spirituality and God knows what. But true humility
that I could feel before another human being would not
come. I went before great gurus with millions of followers
and famous people who were worshipped and was sickened
by the gullible acceptance of disciples and the stupidity
of even scholars and learned people who were novices
in mysticism. The Guru really had a supramental task if
he was to cut through my intellect and my image of what
a true master should be.

I knew he had something, some magical quality that I had
seen work with people quite different from my own
temperament. I knew he had some essence which I myself
did not have and which I wanted. I knew he had permanent
grace, that damned elusive pimpernel that I was chasing

139

down all the spiritual alleys like a hungry hound of heaven.

In an earlier experience I had been overtaken by ecstasy while praying in the tomb of Christ in Jerusalem and had surrendered completely. The grace had flowed and tears of joy had flooded my being to the point where I had become selfless. I felt light emanating from my body in deep trance. I lost all consciousness until I heard a large group of German nuns outside the tomb singing. They were pilgrims with pure white faces and auras. I felt trapped, for in my private contact with the discarnate Christ these nuns had surrounded me and I could not get out of this tomb. I felt glad with them in their joyful song but wished they would leave me in my trance alone with the Christ immanent whose presence I could feel as close as my own self. I knew I was in grace because all of a sudden the Mother Superior came forward from her flock and flung herself at my feet grasping out and touching my feet in the most abject humility. I thought in her religious mania she had mistaken me for a vision, with my long face and long hair, standing in bliss in Christ's tomb. Somehow none of this seemed strange because many times I had been told I looked like Christ but I had always taken this as people trying to appeal to my vanity. I reached out and touched her head and blessed her and knew from the convulsion that she had received Christ through me. The grace flowed and I knew unmistakably what that state was. But in two days it wore slowly off.

So here was I again looking for this same experience with an earthly Being. I had tasted grace and I was expecting nothing less from this Guru before I myself could touch the feet of someone, like that selfless Mother Superior had touched mine. But the Guru was also disturbing. He would do things to freak me completely in my undeveloped area of the heart. Just as I was beginning to trust he would perform some arrogant antic or display some peculiar

140

trait that I knew was in me but should not be in him if he was to be my master. Therefore I could not surrender, although in one rash moment of emotional need, when I thought he would give me grace, I had bent down low and touched his feet and got a blessing. I was terribly embarrassed to do this because I could not abide any false humility in myself or others. I remember it felt good but it had not eradicated the blockages to grace and the defects were still there lying deep in the unconscious. I envied those who could surrender so easily to the human form. It was much easier with dead gurus and Christs.

It was seveal years before I finally surrendered to the Guru and dissolved my separate self-sense into his. He was of the heart and I was of the head and the marriage of the two was intellectually accomplished long before the real union took place. Many times he did the most outrageous things in order to get me to feel beyond my own experiences and see beyond the beyond. I have pity on those who have a big head and a big ego because I know how subtle that deceiver is and how it denied me grace when my heart cried out for it to manifest in me. I would notice grace in simple people and wish I could be ordinary like them. I had an investment and was attached to being someone special. I could see that the secret image behind many would-be teachers was this same feeling of self-esteem. I knew I had to conquer every shred of it but repeatedly I slipped and the Guru did not spare my feelings; in his super-subtle way he never confronted me directly but would always enact some scene supposedly at his own expense.

I remembered that shortly after I had touched his feet I met Raynor Johnson, the physicist turned mystic. We were the only westerners invited to this conference on science and spirituality at Patna and I was struck with his simple humanity. A master of a college and a physicist,

141

Conference on Science and Spirituality, Patna, 1961.

he had come to India with his wife, like myself seeking answers and a great master. The previous day I finished taking photographs of the Guru and the Johnsons with myself and this morning we were going over to meditation. I was feeling a little perturbed because the Guru somehow had introduced me as a disciple and I had not officially in my mind been that humble yet. Sure, I had touched his feet but that was not a complete surrender for me. It was just something external that I had done in one of those blind moments when you hope something will happen but it doesn't until you are really ready.

That morning I had also met a Krishnamurti disciple who had sat at Krishnamurti's feet for many years and decided to leave him because he never said where it was at. Now, I thought, here is a chance to tell this person I have found someone who really knows and says just the right thing at the right time for everybody. I said the fateful words, "My Guru is really there," feeling a little pride. Whenever I used the words, "my Guru" I noticed that when I owned him he would do something that would make me want to disown him. Yet he had just called me his disciple so I slipped into this attitude of secret pride and invited this person to come along to the meditation to meet the Guru, the greatest Guru, the one I was travelling with, who would eventually give me grace and of course deliver what Krishnamurti could not.

At the meditation I noted with satisfaction that Raynor Johnson and the Krishnamurti disciple were present. A short discussion arose as to who should lead the meditation amongst these yogis and spiritual delegates. They quickly picked the Guru and I was elated. You see, I thought, you made the right choice of Guru, they all picked him as the top spiritual vibration. I looked across at the Krishnamurti disciple with a knowing look as if to say, "Now you will really hear some wisdom." I beamed

143

knowingly at Raynor Johnson who must have wondered why I was feeling so pleased with myself. The Guru asked us to form a circle and instead of humbly sitting in it like the rest of us, got up and sat down in the perfect pose in the middle, with considerable adjusting of robes and what I thought was a strange lack of humility. It was disturbing. I thought, "Why not just calmly give the meditation instead of making such a special scene?"

I was not prepared either spiritually or emotionally for what followed. The Guru started to huff and puff in some breathing exercise and I thought, "Why is he doing that? He does not normally make such a song and dance act. Why doesn't he be quiet and lead the meditation?" because all the people here did not need instruction, they were people who had been on the spiritual path for years. I felt definitely embarrassed for him and for me.

I opened my eyes to watch and suddenly he keeled over on his side gasping and looking as though he had got into some trance and he was uncontrollably twitching like I myself did when I was in private communicating with the Devic energies. "But," I thought, "I do not do this act in front of others and any great yogi would always be able to shut off some of the power instead of writhing helplessly on the floor with it." I immediately wanted to disown him as my Guru and was ashamed. In my mind I said, "When this Guru can just meditate properly I will come and meditate but right now I am better off meditating alone." I looked round at the rest of the circle who had all opened their eyes. I was so embarrassed that this was my Guru that I wanted to sink through the floor. On half the faces there was a questioning look and the other half was saying, "What's the matter Guruji?" and some with a look of compassion rushed forward to the center and cradled his head in their arms like they knew the spirit was so powerful in this man that it had made him silly and delirious.

I could hardly stand it. Could he not control the spirit if it was that powerful and just filter enough through so that we could all meditate in peace? I am sure some thought he was having a heart attack and murmured something about a doctor. But I was in touch with only one feeling— my own embarrassment and ego sensitivity. What would Raynor Johnson, a professor of physics, be thinking about such self-control? And whatever would the Krishnamurti student be saying inside about my critical powers of judgement?

I turned to one of the organizers of the conference from the Sri Aurobindo ashram, sitting on my right, with an appealing look for an explanation of this strange behavior. He looked at me and said in a very superior voice, "A lot of ego-mantics going on." That did it! I got up and excused myself and said, "I will meditate when all these antics have finished," and stalked out of the room, not only hot under the collar but disappointed, humiliated, and my ego in no end of a turmoil.

I cooled off during the day and avoided contact with the Guru until afternoon when I could not avoid sitting with him in a group. I did not really want to be seen too close with him. I felt like Peter disowning his Christ! Who me, a disciple of the Guru? No, just a temporary companion on my way round all the gurus of India, said my ego. The Guru leaned over to me with such sweetness and a twinkle that I was nearly melted but I was not going to fall for all this nonsense again. My trust had been betrayed. I was still smarting from being so dumb in the eyes of others.

He looked at me as though he was trying to say something. "What happened to you in meditation?" he asked. "Was

145

there something wrong with you that you had to walk out?" he said rather pointedly.

I was astonished. He should have been asking himself what had happened to himself in the meditation and here was he addressing me as if he had done absolutely nothing unusual. Then I remembered how I had left him with eyes tightly screwed up shut and his body jerking uncontrollably on the floor. As he leaned over I began to recall the scene in very clear detail. I thought, "How could you see me walk out with your eyes closed writhing on the floor like a cobra snake?" But he kept smiling and said, "I am sorry you missed it. These people here have a lot of compassion and heart."

I leaned over to the organizer who had said, "Ego mantics" in such disgust. I said, "How was the meditation this morning?"

He said, "Oh, after you left Guruji got himself very quickly together and the meditation was fantastically high. Everyone had a great experience."

I could not believe it. Had he done that deliberately just because I had boosted him up as my own personal find? Did he know I was almost boasting about him just before that meditation? Did he know that I was worried that Raynor Johnson would identify me on that photograph as a disciple? He had done it again. He had penetrated my ego sensitivity. He had got below my protective shield of knowledge and power. He had put me through that whole scene and risked being judged by all these critical people, but the only one who had actually judged him was me! I felt terrible. Embarrassed on one hand and exposed on the other as proud and unforgiving with no compassion for an old man who could have been going through a heart attack. What use was all my knowledge, my experience of grace in Christ's tomb, my discoveries of new methods of spiritual enquiry, and all my self-esteem if I could not humble myself before fellow man?

I did not know then that twelve years would pass before I could find this humility and that when I finally did surrender to him he would be as dead as the body of Christ. I could not know the agony it would cause me that in my blindness to his ways, I had not seen his true Self before he died. Twelve years later I was standing at the mirror in a friend's apartment in New York and suddenly I saw the Guru's full being looking out of my own eyes. I knew that look! It was as though he were standing there facing me just as he had done that day I had left the meditation, when his eyes had twinkled and he had smiled so sweetly. I remembered that moment of intense ego embarrassment when he had keeled over and writhed in bliss, unaware as a child just born, and how I had disowned him and run away. Now he was inside me looking back at me from the mirror, and I felt the pain of my own arrogance, the pity of my long battle with the messianic search for perfection.

I felt joyful at having found him, but the crushing remorse was as powerful as the joy. I had been waiting for something to conquer my heart before I could surrender—something so awesome, great and magnificent that I could be lifted up and inspired by its light. I had known that the Guru had the power to humiliate me but did he have the power to raise me up? Not until I had conquered in myself the proud ego which had made me expect of him what must come only from myself—only then, when he had come alive in my heart and looked out of my eyes, could I see him as he really was.

THE SEER

Divine light shines within all things
and lights them up with its own glory,
but we do not realize this.
Only when we see the power of consciousness
to limit perception, are we ready
to see the Divinity in all that is seen.

You create all that is around you
by the divine light of your own mind.
Thus Christ says to all beings,
"Ye are the light of this world."

The eye of the intellect
objectively scans the creation
and lights up multiplicity with understanding.
But the divine power of consciousness
is the seer.
Through eyes of love
Divinity beholds itself in all things.
This is why the scriptures say, "Thou art that."
The seer and the seen are ONE.
You are the self of all.
He who created us looks out of our eyes
and sees nothing but Himself.
The environment is total space
full of Consciousness.
The total mind is all around us.

When you are ready
you will humble yourself before its glory,
kneel before its primordial light,
surrender in the depths of space
to your Self.

THE PRESIDENT'S LAST WORDS   13

Gandhi inspired many people to spiritual and social action.

The Guru was a highly respected person in India, a sort of maverick guru in the sense that he had the ear of all the top people but didn't care whether he had any disciples or not, important or otherwise. And several times he kind of blessed me and said, "India is yours; India is in the palm of your hand." It was like the world was all sliced up in pieces and he had India in his pocket and here it was for me. And it was a strange feeling but wherever I went in India, the doors would just fly open for me.

Several years after I left India, I went to dinner with two healers, Ambrose and Olga Worrall, who are now quite famous but in those days were just healers in Baltimore. Francis Woidich was a medical doctor and he wanted me to meet them. Olga was clairvoyant, but she had told him beforehand, "I've got a cold and when I've got a cold I can't see anything." He said, "Christopher is not coming for that but just because I want him to know you." But when I walked in the door, she said, "Oh, oh, I didn't think I'd be able to see anything today but right now I'm experiencing very powerful vibrations. Two people just walked in with you and they tell me that you have India in the palm of your hand."

I was surprised, since those were the very words that the Guru had said to me when I was in India. She went on, "They say Mahatma Gandhi is working for you and organizing all your appointments and connections. One of these two men is saying to me right now, 'How do you think these appointments get made without you doing anything?" It was true. I never made an appointment. They all got made for me. "The second man was showing her a big golden key. "He is the one who opens doors for you," she said. It had been my philosophy for a long time that when I went to a place, if the doors didn't fly open, if there was the slightest resistance, I walked away.

150

I never take much thought about psychics, but I must admit I did get received by a lot of key people, particularly in India. One time I recall about thirty spiritual leaders turned up at Patna for a conference sponsored by the Aurobindo ashram and the Gandhi Peace Foundation. About a week after we arrived for the conference we were told that Dr. Rajendra Prasad, who was our host, was seriously ill and could not attend the session as he had hoped. A medical team had been sent to help and we were told it was impossible to visit, and all communications had to be through doctors. Once he knew that the Guru was here, however, he insisted on getting his daily blessing and so the Guru visited him every day during the conference for a short time.

I had read one of his books before coming to India as he was a very close disciple of Gandhi, through whose influence he had become the first President of India when the British Raj handed over sovereignty to the Indian republic. So I was anxious to meet him even more than I was Mr. Nehru. Although Nehru was a world statesman he did not have a long spiritual background like Gandhi and Prasad.

One day I got a message that I should come along with a group of people from the ashram campus for an audience with the President. About ten people came over to the Prasad residence, but the doctors came out and said we should wait while a decision was taken among them, because the patient had taken a turn for the worse. The verdict came in about an hour, no visitors were allowed except that the President had made a special request to see me and know about my work. I could not believe it! How did the President know about me? Then I realized that the Guru was already in there as he had been every day and must have mentioned my work for world unity to him. I had formed an organization in 1960 called "Framework for

151

Unity" which was to publish a book of people and organizations working throughout the world for peace and world government. Through lack of funds, we never did get the book printed, but all the material was eventually edited and the research done. The Guru must have somehow told him because I myself had told no one at the conference what my real work was about.

I went into the waiting room and a very officious doctor came up and gave me a list of instructions. I could be in the group around the bed with the President's closest friends but was not to talk to him as things were very critical. At the bottom of the bed there was an empty chair and another doctor beckoned me to sit down and said, "We have instructed him not to speak because he is very weak." I sat watching his brown face as he lay half sitting up on a special bed with the Guru sitting by the bedhead to one side.

Suddenly the President's eyes snapped open and he said in a weak voice in front of all these people, the doctors and family, "I would have liked to have got to know Mr. Hills better but I have been instructed not to speak. Could you come over and tell me about your work as I am very interested."

I looked at the doctors as I got up from my chair. They all shook their heads as if to say not possible. I hesitated but the Guru beckoned me to come up to the bedside. The President held his hand out on the sheets and motioned with his eyes to take it in my hand. It felt very weak as I looked at his misty eyes. The doctors were frantically waving at me to leave the bedside. He looked at me very intently and said in almost a cracked whisper, "It is a pity that I am too weak to talk with you, but I wanted to say how much I appreciate what you are doing and to give you my blessing to continue, whatever happens." He squeezed my hand as he said the last words and I opened my mouth to make some reply, but I saw his eyes glaze over and his mouth fall open as he lost consciousness. I looked down at my hand, it was still tightly squeezed and I had to unlock his fingers as the doctors came and shooed me away. They now wanted the whole room cleared of people.

Later they told me he never did regain consciousness and that he had passed away. So his last words were said to me and with his dying breath the first President of India had blessed the work of an Englishman who had made India a second home. I could see later on that several people in the ashram were unhappy that they too had not been at the deathbed. Some had resented that the President's last words should be given to a foreigner. They almost implied I had pushed myself in at the last minute. But I had been very reluctant and it was the Guru who had beckoned me to come over to the bedside.

Ten years later when I had done exactly what Rajendra Prasad had done in getting another group of yogis together, I was giving the opening address at the government's huge Vigyan Bhavan, before a worldwide selection of 800 yogis, 50 western scientists and about 2000 enthusiastic sympathizers. I remembered Rajendra Prasad's blessing on my work at a time when I had no idea that I would myself become the President of a World Conference on Scientific Yoga. I smiled and kept quiet about it, for invisible forces had seemed to bring it about.

After the original steering committee tried to sabotage the huge conference, I felt very appreciative of the positive efforts of people like Dr. Atreya, formerly provost of Benares Hindu University and noted translator of yogic texts. In this picture he is about to give the inaugural address.

WHAT IS GOD?

The universe exists as two states of Being
in one creation
replicating its evolution.

One is the throwing out stage
of manifestation
and the other is the potential state
of the total Being
which is the unmanifest state.
All that is manifest in creation
arises out of its potential state.
Every manifested state
is the beginning of the next higher
potential state of Being.
All that exists NOW
in the creation
is the lowest potential state
of all that is potential and unmanifest.

All that is existing,
from the nuclear heart of every atom
to the radiation of every sun and star,
vibrates together in these two states
which are interdependent,
interpenetrating
and eternally present.

The potential of the unmanifest whole
is locked up in every part which is manifest.
Every part which is manifest
contains the total potential state.
They differ only in their intensities.

Human love and God's love
are in the heart of all that is manifested.
and in all that is yet to manifest the intensity of life.
Everything which is potential in the universe
expands in the completing of this love.

All that is manifest
arises out of its potential state.
All that is high potential
takes centuries to manifest in human life
and millions of years in cosmic life.
All that is of low potential
takes but a few seconds to manifest.
The lower the potential
the greater the speed of replication.
The lower the potential
the greater the speed of communication.
All physical hitting
is communication at its lowest
and fastest and shallowest.
All spiritual communication
of the highest potential states
is slow, deep and penetrating.

All of nature repeats itself
in cycles of higher and lower potentials.
The time intervals
between the manifested state
and the potential states
depend on the intensity of the potential.

All low intensity has little potential
and will manifest soon and penetrate little.
All high intensity will have the greatest
potential but manifest over long intervals
of human history
and penetrate deeply.

Why is this?

The universe exists in two states of Being:
the manifest state
which vibrates in consciousness
as the creation;
the potential state
which vibrates as consciousness itself,
making up the ground state
out of which all manifest states arise
from the total potential state of the universe.

Every potential state
is the ground state
and the pre-existent state
of all that is manifested.
Every potential state arises
from the previous manifested state.

What you manifest NOW
is the beginning of the next potential state
in the higher octaves of life.

Out of the passion of your higher potentials
will come the quality of your manifestations
over long periods of time.

God's wheels grind slowly but fine.
High potential moves slowly but deep.
High spiritual potential penetrates slowly
but is certain and lasting.

To overcome inertia in high potential states
patience must be learned and then lived.
He who would learn the patience
of his highest potential state
must learn to love more,
love deeper and love longer.

As we learn to love
so do we grow.
As we learn to grow
so do we know.
As we learn to know
so we do.
As we do
so we live.
As we learn to live,
Truth manifests.
As we learn to manifest Truth
Christ incarnates as Love.

THE BODI TREE   14

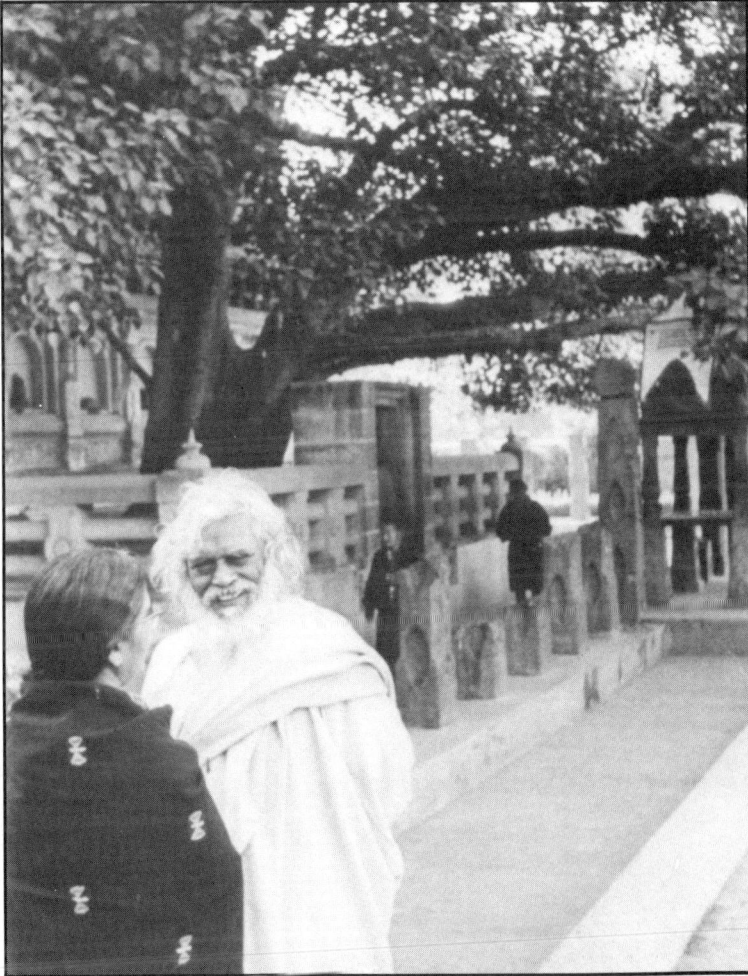

The Guru stands under the canopy of the Bodi Tree at Bodi Gaya.

The Guru at Bodi Gaya.

Attending the conference on "Science and Spirituality" in Patna, at the Ashram of Rajendra Prashad.

I was in Patna for the conference on science and spirituality. The purpose of getting science together with the spiritual realms of investigation was to dissolve the seeming barriers between them. A group of Indian scientists were invited to meet a group of spiritually active people working for the coming new age. This was in 1962 and now, years later, I look back through the lens of time and see how slowly mankind moves towards the real science of the spirit. The probing of one's own consciousness is a continuous process of discovery where science and spirituality overlap, where the scientist and the yogi must be present in the same person.

It seemed quite remarkable that my first materialization of matter from the world of the spirit took place in the presence of a scientist and a yogi. I was thirty-six and had been studying physics for six years. Doctor Sanjiv Vinekar was the director of the scientific research department at a leading yogic hospital at Lonalva near Poona. He had been trained as a medical doctor and was visiting Patna to deliver a paper on the activation of the kundalini energies which he claimed to have measured as they rise through the human body. At the conference he showed his results which he said had been traced by making electrical measurements of biophysical energies with standard scientific equipment. The scientist in me was rather skeptical because I knew how easy it is for religious people to fool themselves and attribute to God almost anything that could happen through natural causes. However, when he brought out his sketches of the path of the kundalini which he had mapped out electrically by carefully following the Sanskrit descriptions set out in certain ancient yogic texts, I began to get excited.

I had had an experience at the age of twelve and thought that everyone had similar experiences. When I saw the drawings I instantly recognized that this was the experience which had happened to me as a boy spontaneously while I was tickling trout among the bullrushes of a river one Sunday morning. I was hating choir practice so much that I decided to play hookey and go out into the fields and woods, and it happened that I had my first psychic contact with another time dimension all those years ago. But I didn't understand it and I knew I couldn't tell anyone so I pushed it into the unconscious. Now I was flashing back, as Doctor Vinekar explained that all he had done was to measure the bioelectric currents at the points where the ancient sages and clairvoyants had said the chakras or psychic electricity centers existed. He assured me they had done it on a number of yogis while they were in a deep state of trance. He had hooked up a whole range of sophisticated apparatus from EEG's for brainwaves to EKG's for heart muscle spasms. He had measured skin resistance, breath exchange between the oxygen and carbon dioxide cycles and even taken x-rays of essential organs such as the stomach wall to study its muscular tension. He had watched the movement of smooth muscle in the intestines and a host of other measurements while yogis went into trance. His method was to bury them in sealed pits for several days at a time so there could be no tricks. A skeptic after my own heart!

I was astonished! Alpha rhythms and delta rhythms had only just been discovered in the West, and the physiological reactions of the brain to psychic energy were completely new discoveries. Even now, years later, when everyone has an alpha rhythm machine or a biofeedback skin resistance meter at home, the degree to which he took his scientific work has not been matched to my knowledge.

There was so much more that we did together later, but at that time I was excited to share the results of my own research with someone who had been scientifically in- vestigating the psychic effects of kundalini from a physiological basis for over ten years. Furthermore he told me that the government of India, headed by Pandit Nehru, had been financing the research for several years. The ashram he had joined as a boy had trained several doctors like himself in regular medical schools especially to do this work on kundalini. I was amazed that they were not a bit interested in putting it in the public domain apart from publishing in their yogic hospital journal.

The prospect of manifesting kundalini energy fired my enthusiasm greatly and Doctor Vinekar invited me to Bombay and Lonalva to meet his guru and to bury me in a sealed pit and test my brainwaves in deep trance. Apparently I was to be nothing new as he had already tested over a thousand yogis of varying abilities so they would have a good idea of any mental tricks I could do. I was fascinated and wanted to become part of this research since I had been a recluse from 1957 onwards at my own mountain-top laboratory in the Blue Mountains of Jamaica, developing methods of detecting the chakra energies with electrical sensors of a different kind. Here was the chance to verify and learn from someone who was both a scientist and a yogi. Here was someone who did not believe in making a name for himself by publishing results, but quietly handed on his achievements to the guru whom he served.

I began to have some doubts because most of the ashrams of India were unscientific and did not even have electricity so could not operate chart recorders and EEG recording machines. Would this be another wild goose chase? I had been to so many places which they said were scientific, only to find no proofs. Everywhere I went all they could offer me were the 2000 year old texts of the sages of ancient days which spiritual India had been coasting on and which I could read myself without any help. I wanted physical concrete proof, something that would give me confidence that this whole fantastic trip was more than scriptures, gurus, promises, words and wild goose chase. Was this *real* or was it just fudging the results to fit the ancient texts? I resolved to visit his yogic hospital and participate in his research.

While I was still talking with Doctor Vinekar, someone came up and said that the famous physicist, Raynor Johnson, and a few other scientists who were attending the conference wanted to visit Bodi Gaya where Buddha had been enlightened 2500 years before. I had always wanted to sit under the Bodi Tree and try to experience what it would be like to annihilate time and psychically contact the mind of Gautama Buddha as he sat under that tree so many years before Christ. I asked Doctor Vinekar if he knew anyone locally who could lend a car so that we could go there and share expenses. He said he would like to come too but I had already thought of taking the Guru who was here at the conference with me. Could the scientist and the holyman get along? If the scientist was as skeptical as I was, would he judge the Guru if he did one of his bizarre acts out there under the Bodi Tree?

The physicist Raynor Johnson had to return the same day for a speaking engagement at the university and so we would only have a short time and then have to leave again. We decided to go in separate cars. Doctor Vinekar knew a friendly ashram right close to the temple where he knew they were interested in scientific research. I went to invite the Guru to come along and show us the ancient University of Nalanda and the more interesting holy places and temples along the way, since it was a long drive of about 130 miles. He smiled knowingly and said Bodi Gaya was a very important place for me especially and that he would certainly come.

We arrived in late afternoon and walked round the temple ruins and visited the lama in charge. A vast number of

164

Tibetan lamas who had escaped from the Chinese oppression were always around, as Bodi Gaya was the most important pilgrimage for Buddhists. I saw one man crawling along on his belly and asked what he was doing. He said he had vowed that if ever he got to Bodi Gaya he would crawl seven times around the seven places where Buddha meditated after his enlightenment, which surrounded the Bodi Tree for about a mile. Seven miles on one's belly, I thought, what good could that do except wear out his lama's robes!

As we got closer to the temple door I noticed about fifty lamas all doing press-ups on shiny boards with a cushion which slid up and down under their hands. I was told these were prostrations and that some would do several hundred thousand to obtain merit, all of which was then surrendered to the Buddha. I wondered what the Buddha needed a hundred thousand press-ups for. Surely these disciplines were more good for exercise and keeping the internal organs in good shape than for achieving such pseudo-overt prostrations of humility. Doctor Vinekar shared my skepticism but said there was a scientific explanation for what they were doing. I decided not to judge them in their naive belief that such physical exercises and self-suggestions were a valid way of conquering the ego. We walked past them and sat down to meditate inside the temple with Doctor Vinekar on my left and the Guru on the right.

Everything was very quiet inside; monks were meditating on the marble floor at the feet of a great golden Buddha, and some sweet sandalwood was burning on the shrine altar. The situation was perfect for meditation and we had got into the front row. Fifteen minutes went by. Suddenly there was a great shout of OM and I looked round and there was the Guru bellowing his head off at the top of his voice. My first thought was, whatever will all these lamas and monks think in this quiet place? I looked around at them; they were still meditating. Then the Guru gave me a big slap on the shoulder and he was off again at the top of his voice, this time on a different note. He signalled me to join in and with a little embarrassment at making such a din in such a quiet holy sacred place, I went up the scale with him as he boomed and shrieked with everything he had got. I visualized all these lamas outside doing a hundred thousand press-ups and thought inside my head, "This Guru is just as half crazy as they are; fancy going through this bizarre screaming match in front of a huge golden Buddha," and I got the strange impression that he was trying to bring the whole universe down on us around our ears by shouting these deafening OM's.

We left the temple for a nearby ashram before the dark fell and Doctor Vinekar introduced us to the yogi in charge of the Samanwaya ashram of Vinoba Bhave whose brother was the resident manager. He assured me we would be welcome to do scientific research at this ashram. I looked around as the dusk was falling and was given an oil kerosene lantern to take into our room. Three cots without any bedding were on the bare concrete floor. They were the only objects in the room. We ate some food and decided to turn in early so that we could go back to the temple the next day and spend some time imbibing the strong atmosphere of timeless devotion to the Buddha.

The Guru turned over on the webbing of his cot and was asleep in a flash. Doctor Vinekar and I talked a while and then about 9:00 p.m. we dozed off. About two hours later I woke with a strange feeling. The moon was full and everywhere was bathed in brilliant moonlight which almost looked like daylight. I was being impelled by a strange force to get up and walk around so I put on my clothes and decided to go for a walk.

The roads were deserted and a weird empty feeling was abroad that night, as if I was here at the end of all life on the planet. There were no pilgrims and I decided to walk back to the temple about two blocks down the road which was brilliantly lit in the silvery light of the moon. I left the Guru and Doctor Vinekar sleeping. The air was very still, like the pause before a hurricane. I came into the temple grounds and saw the huge Bodi Tree at the back of the temple and it seemed to beckon me. I went and sat down underneath it by its trunk and placed my hand against it and talked to it, while thinking in my head that this was all full moon madness. Not a soul stirred and I had the entire temple and its grounds to myself. I asked the tree and its ancestors who had known the vibration of the Buddha to communicate it to me while I meditated under its branches and very soon I lost all consciousness of where I was.

I found myself meditating as if I was inside the Buddha 2500 years ago. He had sat down in this same spot after practicing every conceivable discipline of yoga in order to get enlightened and nothing had worked. He had fasted, he had studied, he had done fire breathing, he had made love in a dozen different Tantric ways and nothing had worked in a dozen years. He had said to himself as I said to myself at that moment, "I am going to sit in this same spot until something happens. I am not going to get up from this spot until I am enlightened." I felt identified so closely that I made the same vow. They would find me here the next morning or days later, because I was fed up with running around doing experiments with light and color and fiddling with a thousand bits of equipment trying to objectify the spiritual energies. I was going to stay there until the same thing that happened to Buddha, whatever it was, happened to me. If necessary I would die there through lack of food or exposure, but I was going into deep trance and would not come out again until I got the Buddha's contact.

I don't remember how many hours passed but suddenly there was a loud blast of sound that seemed to come from inside and outside at the same time. I jumped, it seemed, a few feet in the air, and I opened my eyes. The moon had gone below the horizon and it was almost dawn and this blast of fantastic sound was still going on roaring around the sky. It was as if the sound was a huge person running across the sky, quite different from thunder although it was as loud as a clap of thunder or a stroke of lightning hitting the next block. This sound was a cross between ten thousand railway trucks rattling across the sky and a musical sound produced by a fog horn, yet it was indistinguishable from my own awareness. It was like a hallucination because it was like nothing ever heard before, yet I checked on my mental state and remember distinctly how clear my mind felt. In fact this clarity was the feeling of mindless perception, as if I knew somewhere what this was all about. With a great shout of some cosmic being I had woken up to a super clarity which could contact anyone's mind at any time in history. I was the Buddha, I was sitting inside the One and yet there was no "I" saying this. To say "I" seemed strange, like a separation. The minute I thought "I am experiencing this," it seemed unreal. There was no "I" present to tell any difference between myself and the sound, or between myself and the Buddha of 2500 years ago or anyone else in the various monasteries around me. I was one with all lamas and pilgrims and I just knew that the Buddha had heard that same blast across the night sky. I was feeling very calm and it did not seem to matter whether I got up or stayed. I had been sitting there for 2500 years in my being, and the fact that it was a Bodi Tree made it no different from any other tree or any other body. All that I was experiencing

was a cessation of the self sense and so I continued to
meditate with that sound still ringing in my ears. I was
curious, what was that fantastic noise? Was I all right
or had I died, or what? Yet I knew, and smiled inwardly
for I had the whole of Buddha's temple to myself. The
daylight started to come and I could sense that magic
moment when the sun would come over the horizon even
though my eyes were shut.

Then suddenly it happened again, but this time much
weaker, like a great trumpet being blown with a deafening
roar or like an enormous elephant trumpeting to his
herd. I knew that someone else had heard that sound
and copied it. This time it was a huge trumpet some lama
was blowing from the Tibetan ashram next door. This
sound was coming into my ears and I knew the difference.
The first sound was some actual phenomenon and no
human could have made it happen. A glow came over me.
Other people knew about it. Someone must know what it
was for them to build a trumpet and get exactly the same
note. I meditated on, and about 8:30 in the morning I
opened my eyes slowly and standing in front of me were
Dr. Vinekar and the Guru. People were passing by and
the pilgrims had begun to pray at this sacred spot and I
felt they resented me sitting right plumb where they wanted
to leave their offerings of flowers.

Dr. Vinekar said, "We were looking for you at the ashram.
What happened?"

"I heard a great sound in the sky. It was awesome," I said.
Dr. Vinekar looked at me skeptically.

"What was it like?" asked the Guru with a funny smile
on his face.

"It was like a thousand echoes all coming back from ten thousand things bumping and crashing into each other across the sky," I said.

The Guru said, "That is called a Mega Om and that is a gift to you from God." I thought, "A mega what?" The Guru looked at me and said, "You have just experienced the Super-sonic Cosmic Sound of creation which is still ringing on throughout the universe in eternal time. You are very fortunate because there are seven kinds of OM and that Mega Om is the supreme sound of the One. Come let us go round the seven other spots where the Buddha meditated and see what you can experience from them."

We walked to the first of these spots which can only be described as a little brick and stone cubicle no bigger than the space in which a man could meditate with a statue of a Buddha in front of him. I went inside while the others waited outside the open doorway. It was exposed to the sky and about six feet high. I got a distinct impression that someone else beside Buddha had spent his whole life meditating in that spot whose vibration was as high as the Buddha himself. I tuned in and thought what a high energy was there. I took out my pendulum to check its date. The sixteenth century! The reading came out 960 degrees, using Buddha as one thousand degrees of consciousness. I thought inwardly that the life of devotion of this holyman, whoever he was, was equal to any of our western saints.

A thought came to me. I wondered if this power could materialize a dorje for me. I knew there were certain lamas who could produce a metal dorje from the sky. These dorjes were called thunderbolts and could materialize out of nothing during high meditations. Some of these dorjes had been passed down for centuries and held in the hands of a successive chain of high incarnate lamas who chanted over them for years and years and charged them up with psychic force. I began to think it would be nice if one of those would fly out of the sky and land in front of me in this very high vibration.

Then I remembered. I had been gathering some precious stones wherever I came across some cheap bargains and I had already purchased some rubies which I kept in a small purse in my wallet. The idea was that when I left India I would find twelve key people who would manifest the New Age and present them with a precious stone so that they could all be tuned together in different parts of the world. I had already got four so I took them out of my wallet and spaced them out in front of the statue of the Buddha in front of me hoping that another eight would appear by magic. I closed my eyes and prayed hard. When I opened them again I looked at the four rubies in front of me. They were still there just as I had left them. But in a straight line across in front of them were sitting twelve perfect little stones with a hole drilled through them, as if they had come from a Mala, a necklace rosary. I was flabbergasted and counted them; sure enough it was exactly twelve. I picked one up and held it in my hand. I waved the pendulum over it and got a reading of 960 degrees. This must have belonged to a great saint who meditated here, I thought, who has materialized twelve sacred stones instead of precious rubies.

Excitedly I called Dr. Vinekar and the Guru who were waiting for me outside the cubicle door. "Come and see what has happened," I said, picking up all these new stones and making a handful of them. "Look, I have dated them with the pendulum and they are from the year 1260 A.D.

"How wonderful," said the Guru with a twinkling in his eye.

"You are lucky," said Dr. Vinekar, "Nothing like that ever happens to me," he added, with a look of awe on his face.

I felt extremely pleased. Not only had I got twelve stones to give to those twelve key people, but twelve sacred stones from a saint's rosary nearly as spiritually high as the Buddha himself. How incredible, I thought, that these simple stones should come when I was thinking they would have to be precious jewels to have any meaning to the recipients.

To hear the Mega Om and have a materilization of twelve sacred stones all in one day seemed to be the utmost I could wish for. We went off to look for the head lama to tell him of our good news. The Guru explained what had happened in Tibetan language. I saw a dark look come over the lama's face when he heard the date I had dowsed for the stones. He held his hand out as if I should give them to him, but something told me not to let him put his hands on them or I would never get them back. I closed my fingers around the little pile of stones in the palm of my hand. There were only twelve and none to spare.

A big argument developed between the Guru and the lama. A heated exchange was taking place. I asked what was being said in Tibetan language. He said the lama was angry because I should not take them away, but should have left them in front of the Buddha in the cubicle where they appeared. He was using the argument that they were not my property but belonged to the place. I thought, "Supposing he calls a dozen stout fellow monks, we will soon then have a religious war over these holy relics." So slowly I slunk away, quietly leaving the Guru and the lama arguing in a strenuous debate.

I still keep one of these stones on my Mala. When the current Karmapa first came to the west I happened to go to Vancouver in the same plane. Freda Bedi, an old friend from the Tibetan refugee camp of 1960 who had now become the Venerable Gelongma Sister Kechog Palmo and a translator for his holiness the Grand Lama, introduced me to him. He took one look at the stone and said, "Oh oh," held it in his hand chanting OM MANI PADME HUM. Did he know the vibration in that stone? Did he know how I had come by it? It seemed strange that he would grab that stone in the middle of an airport whilst walking along surrounded by twenty-five attendants and should stop dead in his tracks to say a mantram over it. Did he know too my well-kept secret? The only people who knew what these stones were up 'til then were myself and the other eleven who had received them.

Some of the eleven have manifested their ultimate destiny. Others have fallen by the wayside and have sacrificed that destiny for the immediate rewards of political and worldly recognition. The power of consciousness had materialized twelve stones out of thin air for the atunement of those who would work together to bring the New Age. But the New Age itself did not materialize.

PENETRATING VISION

God is the giver of all good
and the cosmic refiner of all garbage.
Did he not give
the common fly
an attraction
for the putrid stench
of gut-retching meat
rotting in the rubbish?
What makes you pale and puke your heart out
is sweet-smelling goodness
to the miraculous maggot,
who is God glorified
in decaying death.

God is the manure
that grows the finest flower.
God is the beauty of
the supreme hour
that comes to all
who humbly walk the way.
The way of God is strewn
with strange dark nights
of struggling souls,
but the way is also lit
by seven colored lights
of inner fire.

God is in the murmur
of the moving waters
and in the rumbling stones
which speak by the swift river
at Rishikesh.

God is in the crocus
flower by the buried shrines
of Shiloh
and breathes
from the mountainside
at Delphi.

God is the echo of Himself in light
and mysterious
like the sound of the distant cowbells
in the black of night.

God is in London too
floating on the Serpentine
in a small boy's boat
coming home to his heart.

God will reincarnate next
in the poverty of an Indian stonebreaker
whose ego could not break.

God is in the quiet strength
of the peaceful heart,
and looks through eyes
in many lands apart.

When the world is still
and we let it be
without a human will,
then God hurries
to the scene
and gives the heart
its Supreme thrill
to find that God
was ever waiting
from the start.

When God sees Himself in all
we can fall no lower in his sight
for he has been everywhere.
He has looked out of the eyes of harlots
and tempted his own saints.
In blindness he has slain even those very
loved ones that he created.
Has he not visited the dark ocean floor
as often as he's sought out the sun
to warm himself at its fire?
Who taught us to seek him in the sky
and everywhere that's special
and not in what is low?
If we let this go,
God penetrates our heart
with that supreme vision
which all the mystics know.
For inside the seen
God is seeing.
And inside the seer,
he is waiting to reveal
the secret power
hiding in a seed.
He is awake in eyebeams
as the sparkle of love
and asleep in stones
and simple things.

May you see with inner gaze of God's own light
and walk the world with heavenly sight,
humbly shod
with nothing in your heart but God.

THE AGORI

I didn't meet Lama Govinda until 1971.

The Guru was pure but also a powerful presence and until I completely surrendered to him twelve years later, his powerful aura would always have a strange claustrophobic effect on me. Now that he is part of me I do not feel this power but I remember so well the feeling. It was as if my own ego was being swamped with an overpowering admiration on one side of me and the creeping doubt on the other side which he would deliberately foster. He would often do this so that I would make a misjudgement of him and see him as an ego. Then later I would see him do something which I knew could only be done without an ego. I did not tumble to this subtle method of pointing out my own projections until one day in Almora in the Himalayan foothills.

I remember vividly that whenever this overpowering feeling came I would not be able to think for myself in my accustomed self-centered manner. My ego would suffocate since it was used to being number one and with important people at least equal. I would want to run away and escape on the one hand and yet I knew I loved him regardless on the other. At these times I would leave him for a few days on some excuse and visit a new city to pull my ego together again and get back to normal self.

It was a bizarre scene which showed me what he was doing to take on my karma and show it to me. At that time I thought these methods were at a great expense to his own image. Afterwards I saw he did not care a fig about his image. It was the Almora incident which made me see his self sacrifice.

I had come to Almora on a whim because I wanted to meet Lama Govinda. To my disappointment I found he was not even in Almora at that time. We did not actually meet and become friends until 10 years later, but on this first time in Almora he was just a name of someone I thought would be able to give me a spiritual credit rating on this strange and bizarre Guru. I walked away from his house with its view of the Himalayan peaks, wondering what to do with my time and decided to go find the temple places in town and watch the people. I picked a place to meditate near a fountain and a tank where I could also watch human life in all its phases and try to penetrate the hearts of the common people.

I had left the Guru back in Delhi at his cave in the Birla Temple and I was pondering on what his essence was. Suddenly I noticed walking down the street one of the many holymen who pass through on their way to the Himalayas. He had a white shock of hair and a flowing beard and was dressed in pure white and looked just like the Guru. While he was yet in the distance I thought to myself that it was he and was just going to get up and run towards him when I noticed a bunch of disciples following behind like a flock of sheep. I thought, "that couldn't be him." There was something about the way they were walking which I knew the Guru's vibration never encouraged. He would never travel with lackeys or servants because he did not need them. Everything just happened for him, so he would always have a crowd around but it would be a spontaneous group and not look like a posse or church procession walking down the street.

As this holyman and his group grew closer I began to make subtle mental notes on the difference in appearance. His face was almost identical and smiled and looked radiant. I remember noticing how white his bleached robe was washed, worn fresh that morning without a blemish. "That is not the Guru," I thought, "his robes are natural white like the cream color of flannel or the off-white of natural cotton." The group grew closer and came over to the fountain and began to do their ablutions before going into the temple. They washed themselves clean all over even though they looked already clean from washing at the previous temple tank. I noticed how they chanted their prayers and mantrams as they washed and dipped themselves over and over again. It was if they were trying to wash off some sin from their bodies. I got the impression they felt guilty about something and the holyman all this time was encouraging them to keep it up and just when I thought that must be enough washing of their hands and feet, he would dip them in again and say another mantram. I was sitting very close to them when I became aware that someone had come quietly up and was standing motionless by my side watching them.

Then I smelled a strange smell, which I had sometimes associated with hobos and tramps, and which I can only describe as a mixture of dried sweat, old clothes, and stale body odor. I looked round and was horrified. Standing beside me was a member of the dreaded and much feared sect of the Agori who never washed and lived with matted hair in cemeteries and deliberately worshipped death and decay and meditated on garbage heaps. He was almost naked except for the tatters of a loin cloth. His body was covered in dirt and he was exulting in his filth. I was repulsed by the strong black aura which I felt emanating from this living symbol of all that is dirty, filthy and dying. I could hardly stop from holding my nose and he was fully six feet away.

The holyman by the tank noticed him and I saw him turn away in disgust and tell his disciples to put on their robes and get ready to go into the temple. On their way they had to pass fairly close to us to get to the temple entrance. Imagine my shock when this white robed holyman was suddenly confronted by this dark and dirty specimen of humanity who could not have wanted or needed anyone to love him in that state of degradation.

Then a greater shock. While the holyman was yet ten feet away the filthy dark sunburned figure of the Agori shouted out in perfect English, I almost suspected with an Oxford accent of an educated person, in a loud voice so that all the temple devotees could hear, "You there with the lily white robes and so much washing of your guilt away, do you think you are pure?"

The white figure hesitated and stopped as if to turn his followers back and return to the temple later when this unkempt creature was not there. I could see his embarrassment and he took the decision to ignore the shout and continue into the temple. But the Agori was too deft for him. Just as he was opposite he leapt in front of the little party and extended his finger, pointed at the heart of the holyman.

"Why do you think you are pure?" the Agori said accusingly.

The white-haired man looked round at his disciples as if to say, "Why bother to answer such a human specimen?" but his disciples encouraged him and hurled insults at the black Agori. The Agori smiled as if an insult was the most beautiful compliment you could pay to anyone. The more foul the word was, the greater he liked it. After a while the group settled down and the disciples began to beg the holyman to answer him.

"Show him your power Guruji," said one disciple, but the holyman looked a little afraid, because he knew the Agoris did all these things to gain powers and they were known to use them in strange ways in any psychic contest.

The Agori pointed his finger again, "Tell me what makes you pure?" he said in a loud voice for everyone to hear. The pilgrims had begun to crowd round from the temple now and the white dressed holyman had gathered his flock in a tight bunch behind him, many of them also dressed all in pure white. He looked at the Agori with a look of pity on his face.

"All my life I have studied the scriptures and done daily ablutions," he said rather pathetically.

The Agori looked at him, grinning from ear to ear in a sort of devilish leer. "You think that washing in the tank a thousand times will clean your inner guilt away?" the Agori said.

The holyman replied, "We study only what is holy and pure and lead a moral life."

"What is *not* holy?" said the Agori. The white-haired holyman knew he was trapped. If he said one thing was not holy then Brahman could not be in everything everywhere as he often preached. He decided on another tack.

"You are blocking our way to worship the Holy Shakti power."

"Ho Hum!" said the Agori. "It is not I that is blocking your way but your own impurity."

The pure white washed holyman looked at his disciples as if for reassurance before answering. I could not help identifying with his situation. What would this holyman's double back in Delhi have done and said in this situation? I could not imagine him ever being put through this humiliation in front of disciples. But then, I thought, he said he never had any disciples except Himself. Was this the reason that he could not be given embarrassment? I wondered what he would have said to the last statement.

"How do you mean?" said the lily-white holyman playing for time. "What impurity are you talking about?"

The Agori looked at him and said, "Here you are all puffed up, lording it over your disciples, commenting on all their shit, but not able to eat your own."

The holyman recoiled at the word 'shit' and made a face. "I am well known for doing myself what I preach to others."

The Agori laughed uproariously and said, "But there is one thing you are not pure enough to do and that is eat your own shit."

I was shocked at the thought and the holyman looked disgusted as if to say, "How horrible a specimen of the human race you are," with a look of intense loathing all over his face.

My thoughts flashed back to my own baby son who would put handfuls of his own excreta in his mouth if we did not get him to the potty quickly enough. My mother had told me that I did the same and that one day she caught me crawling under the motor car and eating all the black dirty grease from the front axle. I was revolted by the thought, yet I knew that at some time the idea that excreta was dirty must have been severely planted there by adults for babies to stop eating their excreta.

But my attention went quickly back to the drama being enacted before me. Here were the team of guilt washers pitted against one powerful man who saw only beauty in all that is dirty. Could the Agori be suffering from some strange obsession to make all this a religion, or was religion an obsession with the washing away of sin and guilt? I was shocked, disgusted and confused and was watching the expression of utter loathing on the face of the holyman. I became aware that the Agori was also watching the expression and was enjoying it like a great compliment. There was a pause as it was obvious that he was waiting for the loathing to die off before speaking further. The holyman turned to his disciples and made a start as if to pass into the temple, but the Agori shouted, "Wait and see how pure you are," and with that he put his hand down to his behind and excreted into it with a short dramatic crouch. Springing forward with a handful he offered it to the holyman saying, "Here take my offering, it is holy. Eat it and you will be pure." He held it in outstretched hand standing directly in front of the holyman.

The lily white holyman snorted with anger, his mask of holiness now transformed into a picture of undisguised rage. "You evil and filthy demon," he shouted, "you are the living symbol of darkness and I am of the light."

The Agori smiled, "God turns all the world's excreta into light," he said. "When you are pure enough to eat your own shit, you will be pure." And with that he stuffed the handful of feces into his mouth and began to eat it very deliberately in front of the holyman's face until in blind rage the old man brushed past the Agori, not caring about getting his white robes dirty, and ran into the temple with his disciples following sheepishly with looks of sheer horror.

The Agori turned to me and saw my disgust and finished eating his mouthful looking intently at me while he chewed away. I felt his eyes boring through me into my soul. Was he looking for dirt there too, or was he looking for purity? I had the distinct impression he was reading me. I looked at the dirt within myself and thought, "Why does he have this obsession with external dirt if he is pure within?"

I thought that yes, if it was a matter of life or death I could eat my own excreta and particularly that of someone I really loved. As the thought crossed my mind, I saw the Agori smile and the fierce look in his eyes turned to compassion. Was he so pure amongst all that external filth that he could even read all my thoughts? I could not answer. I was very confused and yet I knew I had just witnessed a very important lesson. The washing away of sins and guilt was a common psychological problem. Was religion and our western concern with spiritual and physical purity the other end of this man's obsession? Had I just witnessed two extremes of external and internal purity, or was this some mad dream that I was having in this midday sun? What could be this man's motive for accosting people in this way only to be hated and loathed and feared? Did he have a self-image of purity which did not depend on anyone else's feedback?

I was greatly disturbed and sickened and here was this filthy Agori looking at me and chewing his shit as if nothing was happening. I was scared he would come over to me and start talking. He was obviously an educated person from his English accent. I was freaking now. Supposing he comes over to me and asks me to eat with him? What would I do? What would I say?

I thought about the Guru back in Delhi. What would he do in this situation? The Agori seemed to catch my thought and nodded English style. I thought, that's strange, because Hindus don't nod when they say 'yes,' they shake their heads with a little sideways movement. Was he nodding at my thought of the Guru?

I decided to try a quick experiment and tune into the Guru back in Delhi, and see what he would say if this awful creature came over and said anything when he had finished masticating his excreta. All this is happening fast in my mental computer because I am also wanting to get up and run away from this guy before he decides to come over. I decide that is not the way to resolve the conflict within me and I tune into the Guru a bit harder for an answer. The Agori is nodding again and this time his black aura disappears and a look of intense love comes all over his face and his eyes shine like the Guru's back in New Delhi 500 miles away. I can't believe it. I am not looking at the dirt on this guy anymore; I am looking at his eyes which are on fire with love.

Who is this guy anyway? Is he real or is it some disguise he is wearing? I am still confused. Is this the Guru in Delhi going through another bizarre scene for my benefit? Is he staging this drama to get below my ego which caused me to run away from him 500 miles to get out of his damned overpowering aura? Or is it just coincidence, something I would see anyway with my own powers of perception?

I decide on a further test. If this Agori turns on love in his eyes every time I think of how the Guru would handle this situation, what would he do if I put it all down to my own powers of insight and forgot that Guru back in Delhi? As I thought the thought the Agori's look of intense love suddenly frowned into a look of pure hostility and he turned on his heel and stormed down the road.

I watched him marching away without looking back until he got into the distance. Was he real? Was I really sitting here watching this Agori who had taken his excreta and turned it into love, walk into the Himalayas never to be seen by me again? Whatever he was, the message was clear: that we cannot eat the external shit until we have eaten our own internal shit, and that is how God turns all excreta into light.

What was the lesson? To face the unpleasant, to look beneath the impure, to find love and truth in what man rejects? Was it not Christ who was rejected of men, and was it not truth that was crucified?

TO THE GREAT MUSICIAN

To tune into a great mind
and feel the music flow
from the Supreme Source,
is to experience
the breath of heaven
and the flowing fountain,
pouring from the sacred mountain
in the heart.

To realize the depths
of a great mind
is to feel the presence
which all the mystics
find so unbearably beautiful.
How great and good thou art
who moves as light of the mind
into the depths of heart.

Echo of the master spirit,
the music of a great mind bestows
a virtue on all beings
and opens the soul
to the supreme communion.
And the heart opens to that radiant
love which lies behind
the vibrations of a great mind.

Give me music for the soul
and the universe becomes
one whole world
heaven-high
felt in the breath
of one cosmic sigh.

For in one moment of
cosmic bliss
the goddess with the divine kiss
can find in music
the God of all sweetness.

The crown of life is love,
and if this love is carried
on waves of light and sound,
there is a purity,
some subtle fluttering of angel's wings
that we can almost hear
hovering in the background.
And we experience
these resonances from the Source
with all the force and power
of a moment in the presence
of that One whose notes are ringing
in the silence
as it cradles every sound.
The divine musician's notes
are the feelings called forth by tones
(spoken, sung, chanted, played,
or even rasped)
if they are born out of love.

MEETING WITH NEHRU

16

Mr. Uppadhyaya and Mr. Nehru and I in Nehru's garden just before I left India, 1962.

I had shaved off my beard, cut my hair and was now again in the same western suit I had arrived in. My shoes had seen the soil of India from the most northern Himalayan kingdoms to the southern tip of the continent. I was nearing the end of my stay in India and I was back at the same place I had begun—the guest quarters of the Birla Temple in New Delhi. I was reminiscing about the events and the passing of time since my first day in India at the Guru's cave at the back of the temple yard. The Guru had done his best for me and now the real work on myself was to begin.

I had work to do for the world that had been partly laid aside, and I was not yet clear what direction it should take. The book "Framework for Unity" had given me access to leading agencies of world change and important personalities on the world scene. I had temporarily dis-continued it because I was going through some self questioning as to whether this was an effective way to go.

In my long journey through Europe and Asia I had realized that many of the world's happenings which cause the most sensation, loss of life or oppression, are not really world changing events at all. Prime ministers and presidents come and go. Dictators rise and fall. While in power they strut across the world scene and leave barely a trace when they have gone. Also great enterprises seem to rise and go awry so easily; whole wars which are the talk of the day and sap so much of a nation's vital nourishment, seem to be unnecessary and ineffective in retrospect. Wars of liberation, wars of revolution, end with the opposite result; when the new lords take over, oppression is even a thousand times worse. Somewhere there must be an answer for the world's peace.

Most people were concerned with the immediate problems of getting power, feeding the world, technical aid, education in everyday basic skills. They did not believe that the real problem was to understand the darkness of their own ignorance. But if people in important positions were totally blind to any solutions except their own, how could there be anything called progress? Wisdom did not prevail in the councils of the world. Governments did not search for wisdom but for what is expedient. The clever would always answer, "Who can tell us who is wise? Let us talk of other things." Then I realized that governments had no soul; like big corporations their reason for existence was to satisfy the shareholders or the votes. Furthermore the type of person who could stomach the lies, the methods of electioneering, the promotional campaigns and the sheer waste of money on the advertising media, was insensitive already to the concerns of the wise. No one with sensitivity for subtle Truths and who abhorred mendacity could participate willingly in the politician's manipulative struggle for election to office. Such occupations represent neglect of work upon oneself. The rationalization was always, "We have to do it or we would not get elected." Then having fought hard to get somewhere within the system they were not going to change its basic structures even if they could. They were for change with their mouths, but their nature was not to disturb beautifully arranged apples on the cart. Therefore in essence politicians were powerless to bring about fundamental change.

Some other alternative was needed but no one would risk an untried system. It was a chicken and egg situation. Untried systems like communism ideally appealed to intellectuals and activists but when tried never succeeded without more repression, killing, ruthlessness than before and were self-defeating.

The situation looked hopeless. If only the nations would form a council of non-political wise men that could be fed as a group a stream of insoluble problems that were way beyond the capacity of any politician to solve, then they could give an independent answer as to what is right, not *who* is right. This would only have a moral or ethical power and no government need be bound by its answers. The important words were "if only" yet if only governments would seek alternative answers to insoluble problems, merely asking an uncommitted group for an original answer would give the world some new ideas rather than depending on the conventional wisdom which is the bastion of politics.

But who would be the first to recognize a wise man's group or call it into being? Obviously no group of citizens could set up a council of the wise without being accused of some fundamental bias, either capitalist or communist, conservative or socialist. Was there anyone with such great stature as a statesman whom the world respected enough?

Then I suddenly thought of Pandit Nehru. Here was someone educated in England and respected by the British and most countries as a level-headed statesman who had succeeded in welding together the most diverse political elements of India. Containing a fifth of the world's population with a mixture of castes, religions and philosophies, India could be said to be a miracle of cohesion. Left by the British with solid institutions it had not degenerated then into warring factions.

I was sorry I was leaving India because if we could get Mr. Nehru to call such a world council into being then we could set in motion the idea of each country's sending its most prominent philosophers to such a council. That could be my new mission, to visit all those invisible philosophers-in-waiting. The idealist in me was running wild. Let's have a world center where they could all live and meet to cut through the Gordian knot of ignorance. The armchair philosopher was sitting on his bed in the Birla Temple indulging.

I was musing what to call it. "The Council for Insoluble World Problems," "The Council for Resolving Conflict Creatively," "The Council for Universal Laws of Government," and a dozen other names kept flashing through my mind until it was late at night. How could I see Mr. Nehru? He didn't even know me, although I did know the deputy leader of his party. But I was leaving India tomorrow evening and there was no time for making appointments.

Now I was toying with the idea of staying and seeing this idea of the conflict solving council through, to get it through to Mr. Nehru. I thought of all the preparation one has to do to convince practical politicians that your scheme is not just one of ten thousand ideas which go into the waste basket. I would need to design and print a leaflet to get support, so that the long political chain of command would know I had clarity and was not some time-waster. Before giving me an appointment with Prime Minister Nehru his office would have to know who I was and what it was about.

It was time to turn in and to decide tomorrow whether to cancel my leaving, or to proceed on my visit to other capitals. I had planned to visit and see my long list of citizens interested in world government and paranormal phenomena which had been my fields of action for so many years. I went to sleep with the thought that my days as a recluse were now over; I must be about the Father's business.

It was the next morning and the time was seven o'clock. I lay a while half asleep thinking, "What shall I do?" Suddenly I felt a tug on my shoulder, "Wake up! Wake up!" I heard as I struggled into waking consciousness. It sounded like the Guru's voice inside my head. I sat up on the bed and began to pull my socks on. I was still half-awake as if in deep trance from reflecting on my problem.

Suddenly I noticed he was standing right there in front of me about four feet away. He smiled and said, "Come get up and get ready. You have to see Mr. Nehru at 8 a.m. and his parliamentary secretary will come for you at ten minutes to eight." I never dream but the situation was so bizarre that I thought this message from the Guru most unlikely. I could not believe it. I must be hallucinating! So I rubbed my eyes but he was still there. "You are to go to Mr. Nehru and then my work is finished. I can go now into my samadhi. Be ready at 8 a.m. Bless you."

A short cryptic message like that and the Guru was gone. He dissolved before my very eyes. I jumped off the bed. I could not believe he was not there in person; he looked so real. I ran to the doorway and looked down the long passage. No one there! Strange I did not hear his footsteps. How did he know what I was thinking? A thousand rationalizations crossed my mind. But he looked so real, so convincingly of solid flesh. I could tell every detail on his face and clothes. I could see the special look in his eyes.

I was stunned and did not take it seriously. Going to the Prime Minister indeed! Perhaps I was hallucinating or imagining things and I put it down to a waking dream. Maybe I had eaten some of the dirty uneatable foods which is all one can buy at Indian railway stations. Maybe the results of eating in a dirty restaurant had affected my head. To go to see a Prime Minister with half an hour's notice was just too far out; it was too impossible for the political machine to operate that way. I dismissed the idea and went on getting dressed slowly and then went to wash. Why would a Prime Minister send for somebody unknown to him? It was absurd that the leader of 500 million people sought after by leading statesmen the world over would be seeking a person like me.

As I came out of the bathroom I heard the running feet of a messenger coming down the long passage way. "Sahib! Sahib!" he was shouting excitedly. Before he could reach me he blurted out his message. "Sahib, a taxi at the gate from Panditji. Prime Minister's secretary waiting for you. Come right now. Not to keep waiting please."

I was shocked. It was true then, but how could it be? I was completely mystified. I had not told anyone I wanted to see Mr. Nehru. Until yesterday I couldn't think of a politician whom I really respected enough to want to see him. I hastily threw on my suit jacket and ran to the iron gates of the temple which were still locked for the night. The gatekeeper flung them open and I looked at my watch. It was ten minutes to eight. Incredible. The message was exact.

The door of the taxi opened and a small white-haired man with a gentle face beckoned me inside and introduced himself as Mr. S.D. Uppadhyaya M.P. who had been parliamentary secretary to the Nehru family for over forty years from when Panditji was a child. His father had been governor under the British raj while Nehru was at school in England.

I began to say that for a man of Nehru's age he certainly started work at his office early in the morning! Whereupon he said this would be a social visit, but first I would come to his own house on the presidential estate, meet his family and drink some char (tea) until 10 a.m. Then we could go across and discuss my proposal for a world-wide council of wise men to solve the problems which crop up and cause crisis after crisis between the nations.

I was flabbergasted and went into shocked silence. I had not discussed my proposal with anyone but the Guru, years back when we had first met, and then only in some vague

195

form more like a wish-fulfillment, that it would be nice if it could come true. Was it coming true or was I still having a dream? We arrived at Mr. Uppadhyaya's house and I was treated like an honored guest. It was a rather uncanny feeling that some invisible power was at work beyond my conscious mind.

I took photographs of his family and we shared the beauty of his baby grandson and enjoyed the flowers and peace of his little garden. Then at 10 a.m. we both walked over to the presidential palace which had formerly been the home of the Viceroys of India. It was the White House of India. In the lobby were many people from all over India waiting to see Mr. Nehru and I was told he received whole groups in the garden every morning in order to keep his personal contact with the people. Most Prime Ministers make themselves inaccessible; not so Nehru.

I waited while Mr. Uppadhyaya explained the purpose of my world mission. I had been working out ways to bridge the gap between a person's thoughts and the emotional conflict which was set up in him when confronted by his actual existence. I felt sure there was a scientific answer to spiritual problems.

Nehru agreed that science had never been properly applied to the science of the soul, or the exploration of inner space, and with his western education he was able to grasp some of the concepts behind what we were doing in laboratories in England and other countries in conjunction with the holymen of India. I asked him to help us in our work for the total transformation of human consciousness, so that the world may have peace. "What do you want me to do?" he asked.

I explained carefully that these energies that shunt about the miraculous circuitry we call a human being were

196

capable of being abused like any other discovery. Man since the beginning had used the great power of "Union" until it had become despotism. Man had used religious unity to gouge out the eyes of several Popes and torture those who afterward were made saints, and now he had used the great power of atomic energy to enslave himself to war and armament and become the chief servant of mammon. If it were possible to release the hidden powers in man's own nature how could this in all responsibility be given to an unready world until some world authority or council of the world's wisest men had been set up to implement its creative, and not its destructive use.

Could such an authority be made up from the existing heads of state of this chaotic world? Of course not, for the very destinies of these men were all governed by chancy elections, by almost whimsical happenings on the political scenario which we call the real world of "power" and national glamor. These men had to be the type of men we could trust our lives with and feel safe. We could not let them drive the world bus without looking at the expiration date of their driver's license! On this level of "life" the question of national sovereignty became of no importance. Could he not be the first statesman to set up and recognize such a World Council which could advise governments? Power could be given with each frame of reference just as we give the court or an arbitration the power to come to a legal and valid decision in any dispute which might extend itself into violence.

He laughed ironically, "I am sympathetic to your idea, but at the moment I am fighting a war to preserve our sovereignty against the Chinese!" He agreed that each democracy was a law unto itself, that it dealt with other countries and other democracies on the basis of autocracy. "How can the nations, particularly the democratic ones, give up any sovereignty?" he asked. "Take myself for example," he said. "I agree with you but this is the job of philosophers not politicians. I am a democrat and there is no politician who can do as you ask because every Prime Minister derives his power in a democracy from the people. Therefore he cannot give any sovereignty away to a world center or to a council of wise men, even if he wanted to personally. No democracy has that power."

We discussed some of the insoluble problems that he would like to pass on to such a body of planetary-thinking men, but he said it was clear that such a set-up would have to come from outside of politics. It was only possible to give some measure of recognition after such a council was set up, just as various countries recognize the International Court at the Hague, the international character of the Red Cross or the United Nations. In his opinion the job of establishing such a body that transcended nationalities could only be done by an authority higher than the Prime Minister of a democracy. He said he did not know of such an authority. "These are problems of the New Age. They are for young people to deal with," he said, looking at me very pointedly, "I wish you success in your undertaking."

Many times the interview with Nehru came back into my mind and I followed events in India fairly closely for the next ten years until I returned in 1970. I had heard from the lips of one of the world's great statesmen an expression of not only his feelings on sovereignty but how firmly entrenched was nationalistic sentiment in the people of India. This made my self-appointed task of working toward world unity and universal government seem like a huge steep-sided mountain that I had set out to climb.

It was my interview with Nehru that spurred me to search for another way, far removed from political systems and even from philosophies of federalism. There would have to be men and women willing to sacrifice their pride and their selfishness. With all their boundaries broken down, they would merge with each other in selfless love and become a prototype group to seed again and again until the whole planet became a garden without gates or fences and without fear. As my spirit rose at the prospect of eventual union and peace, I saw, too, that it could take a thousand years.

BEYOND HUMAN LIMITS OF LOVE

If perfect love,
all human thoughts transcending,
exists beyond our understanding,
can we ever know that love?

Is not perfection itself
a human concept,
a mere opposite thought
to the imperfect?
And what is there
that is imperfect?

For if we look deep
into imperfection
we find the perfect cause of it
is nothing but our own ignorance.
Probe deep into the world of evil
and we find a hidden world
of cosmic law.

Does not evil divide
and destroy that which is not real?
Does not evil crucify truth
that it may be seen
and brought into light?

And what power does evil have
over the real?
All that is phoney and evil
is exposed by the envy of evil ones,
while the good suffers them
in kindness.
The evil one exposes the evil
and reveals the good.

Selfish love betrays the lover
and reveals the true love.
The negative gives
more power to the positive
and forces the perfect love to act.
And what is this act of perfect love?

If love is all around us,
vibrating in the tremendous forces
of attraction
in the nucleus of atom and cell;

If love is in the radiating
heart of the sun
and other giant stars;

If countless galaxies rotate in space,
held together and bound in unity
with the inward gravitating force
of eternal love;

If love is expanding outwards
throughout the whole of space
at the speed of light,
then how do humans know
that all this vast scene
is perfect love?

How can we know the quality of our love?
How do we know that our attraction to others,
our love as humans,
and the overflowing emotion
which consumes the heart,
is really the ultimate good?

Do we gauge the ultimate thing
by the measure of its pain?
or by the height of its ecstasy?

How do we know whether our measure
of love and bliss
is merely one narrow octave
in the spectrum of love
so big that we cannot know
how big is Big?

Expand love out so far
beyond any idea of big
to the big, Big,
to the big, Big, BIG Brahman
who is really BIG,
and all limits are lost.

This is yoga. This is Christ.

Yoga is union,
and union is the limitless
expansion of love
beyond any idea of a lover
or something to be loved.

Who can love in this limitless way?

Only the yogi, the saint, the Christ,
the seeker of the Supreme Self.
For, in total union
there is bliss
emerging from within
utterly transcendent.

THE BLESSING 17

With the Guru and Mr. Uppadhyaya at the Taj Mahal.

We decided to go to nearby Brindaban to visit the "joy permeated Mother."

I was with the Guru and with Mr. Nehru's parliamentary secretary, and the secretary suggested, "Why don't we go and see Anandamayi Ma; she's in town." The Guru said, "Sure, let's go and see her."

We got to the gate of her ashram in Brindaban and said, "We want to see Anandamayi Ma." But they said, "There are about 5,000 people in the ashram, all waiting to see her." People used to have to wait about three or four days just to get a look at her. So they said it would be about three weeks before we could meet her. Everybody was there chanting bhajans, and thousands of people sitting around in states of prayer and what have you. So I was very surprised when the Guru just brushed them aside and walked straight through like a great big battleship with us following in his wake.

He says, "Where's Anandamayi Ma right now?"

The disciple said, "She's in her bedroom in meditation." So the Guru marched up the steps and of course we followed, and everybody was rushing saying, "No, no, no, she's in holiness, she's in a holy state right now talking to God."

The Guru said, "Ah, that's okay, fine." And he walked straight into the bedroom and there she was sitting up in bed. I marched in behind, thinking, "Well this is strange, going into a woman's bedroom without invitation or knocking on the door or anything." He marched straight in.

I expected her to look a bit angry or something, like, "How dare you come into my bedroom when I'm in my meditations talking to God!" But when she saw him, her face lit up like a sun and she said, "Aaahhhhh!" just like that. She said, "Come sit on the bed."

And I thought, "What? a holy woman? making a man sit on her bed?" The Guru sat down and took her hand and I thought, "My God, are these two people in love behind the scenes or what? She's a big guru and so is he."

They talked in Hindi or whatever, some language, and he was telling her about me, so she kept looking at me with those kind of eyes, like spaniel's eyes. And I felt a very holy vibration. She didn't say anything to me specially, but then he said something to her and she got out of the bed and he said to me, "Is there anything you want to ask her?"

I said I'd like to have a blessing, and I put down my head to get the blessing. She took my head and ruffled all my hair up and I felt a wonderful feeling of lightness penetrate right through my head. When I came up I looked into her eyes and I took her hands and we stayed about twenty minutes just holding hands, nothing to say. I felt a very holy vibration and I felt something like energy creeping up my arms, though I wondered whether they were just getting numb from holding them in the same position. A born skeptic, you know, I had to ask the question whether it was holy power or whether it was my muscles getting tired.

Traveling in India with the Guru, I used to see the devotion and devout feelings of the Hindus as they worshipped about 500 different gods. But I never saw the Guru put a piece of that colored stuff on anybody's forehead. I never saw him do one ritual. I never saw him in an attitude of what one would call the traditional style of holiness. He always looked a bit roughed up and his hair was all over the place and his gown was never on properly, and yet there was just something about the man, like he was a natural. He radiated, like beams of light were coming from his being. He never seemed to go in for any kind of stylized holiness whatsoever. It just seemed to come from some inner space. It was no big deal to him, no effort.

And Anandamayi Ma was like that too. Her vibration was like the Guru's, an en-light-ening vibration—so far from all the concepts that people have about holiness. She has a sort of pure holiness, so natural you can actually feel it. It lifts you up. As we left, she came down the steps with us and she walked with us to the gate. "The disciples were right," I thought, "She was in a holy state."

Sri Anandamayi Ma

LOVE IS ITS OWN REWARD

Why do I love
without a love object?
Because the fire of love expands
throwing out itself to itself.
If my breath goes out
it must come in
or there is death.

Do not worry about inhaling life
for the out breath is a radiation
which returns like an echo—
self-governed immortal resonance
re-sounding the cosmic law
of the One I love.

Love is the systole and diastole of life.
To radiate love
gives its own reward.
To give is to receive.
Yet men cannot believe this truth.
What stopped them before,
all the days of their lives,
stops them now and tomorrow
the driving thirst for sorrow.
Will they find what they are looking for?
Or will they get something "spiritual,"
abstract and ethereal,
no use in the Kingdom of Earth.

Wholes and hunches in heaven
are played at cost
and cosmic certainties given and lost,
to find, reversed in heaven's law,
the bonus hidden in the flaw.

Love is stopped now and stopped tomorrow
because men's thirst is more for sorrow.
But this is just the lack of trust,
for sacrifice itself love must
or burst the heart in pain
again and yet again.

The stars give out continuously
but they all receive each others' light.
Love bathes all eternally
in heaven's sight
and radiates through space
in the totality of the dark
endless night.

The cosmic law
can be seen quite plain
in self-centered lovers'
never-ending pain.
Love which does not give
does not live.
The lovers' law embraces all in cosmic arms.
Its magic charms appear as grace.
An invisible embrace
spirals in space
radiating in eternity.
But who can give on a cosmic scale
and never fail.
Giving all
to get the spiral flowing
the cosmic lover
gives without knowing
whether or not he will receive.

That law which gives us birth,
expanding from the universal womb
dies and contracts
into the deepest cosmic tomb.
Death of ego is the start
of life in galaxies
of the heart.

The universal law stands
governing all from stars to deeds.
When spinning galaxies increase their speed
the fire of love expands.

Need becomes seed.
God implants desire
and man begins to aspire.
The soul must learn
to trust the law of giving,
for the effect on the world around
is a reflection of one's heart.
What emanates from the heart
is real.

Transition from heart to matter
causes our thoughts to scatter
and time begins its spiral whirl.

Rotating faster heats dead matter
until its atoms begin to sing.
Humans think this an ordinary thing.
Love radiates through all the shells
and matter in turn repels.
Bodies repelled expand to cosmic rule,
while expanding bodies cool.
Yet man's heart seeks the fire
to fill the hole of cosmic desire
in his yearning soul.

Cosmic cooling integrates all things
while integrating matter spins and rings
with love's sweet sound
and all around
is this same thrust,
creating Adam from the dust.
Calm and cooler rotates things slow
and slow rotation contracts the flow.
Thus man continues stopped in love,
failing to understand this force
when one radiation would change his course.
When man begins to imitate earth
giving and giving for all he's worth,
the cooling balm of love's returning
wells up to quench his deepest yearning.

One huge heart controls disintegration,
accelerates rotation.
Accelerated rotation expands;
expanding bodies cool;
the cooling body contracts;
contraction generates heat;
heat energy creates radiation.
Radiating bodies rotate faster and expand
into space. Expansion cools
in the self-governing Universal system
and the system is the One.

Why does the One radiate love
without an object?
Because the fire of love
throws out the Self to itself
and receives itself with love.
Love is its own reward.

POWER OF
TELEPATHY

18

Was it to discuss light with him or just to experience his light?

One year had passed since I had seen the Guru in India. I had been travelling almost continually giving lectures in London, Los Angeles and New York on Radiesthesia and the transmission of healing energies through color and the use of psychotronic devices. I began to feel a need to see the Guru again but I knew he was in samadhi in the house near Kalighat in Calcutta. My thoughts would go to Calcutta and yet something I could not explain was saying to my inner mind, "If you are truly ONE there is no need to go physically," and another voice would say, "Why go all that way to hear what you know he would say anyway?" But something kept gnawing at the bones of my being.

I remembered the same feeling I had about Einstein. After reading Einstein's own explanation of his theory of relativity I sensed a great Being behind it striving to objectify the spirit. Somehow I saw him as a great yogi in a former incarnation who had been a researcher (Rishi) and who had gone the way of supreme devotion and had then come back to work out his thought experiments with mathematics. This sensing of something great and awe inspiring behind the man caused me many times to want to go and visit him and just experience his being. Many times I made the decision to go to Princeton and see the old man but I always felt such closeness and kinship mentally that I always put off the trip. My inner voice would say, "If you had really penetrated the mind and soul of Einstein you would not have this hankering after this physical meeting in the flesh."

I would on occasions feel the impulse so strongly that I would go to the airline office to buy the ticket and then say at the door, "What would you say to him? He would just think you were another curiosity seeker come to waste his time with nothing special to say." I would turn away from the airline office muttering to myself something to the effect that "Spirit and matter are one," "Spirit and flesh are one," "Who is separate from who in a cosmic mind like Einstein's sitting on the surface of a tiny planet?"

People must have wondered many times when they saw me walk up to an airline door, put my hand on the handle and turn away muttering. Yet this longing did not go away until the hour of his death when it changed to remorse and regret. I remembered hearing the news on the radio and thought, "Now you cannot pay a visit. Would you have gone to see Jesus Christ in the flesh if you had had the chance? Here was a man whose stature comes but once every thousand years and you did not go to his light, but thought instead you could get it all from his books." Regret at missing such a rare spiritual seer into the heart of matter overcame me, and tears would come to my eyes. I knew I should have gone to Einstein just to experience the Being, even though I felt close in the heart, as close as I already felt to Socrates, Bach and Newton. I had always had this feeling of being inside their minds through entering the vibrations of their work which seemed to be interfused with their souls. Whether this is my imagination or true telepathic contact, cannot ever be proved since it is a subjective feeling like love.

After Einstein died I would get this on and off feeling of regret that I had missed a contact on one of the earthly levels of consciousness; it was something akin to one's feelings about the disciples' experience compared to our second-hand hearsay knowledge of Christ. There was no substitute for first-hand direct knowledge, which can take place in a flash between eye and eye, in heart to heart or head to head contact. It is the quality of presence. This quality is transmitted in a voice or even on a tape machine or telephone. I had always had this ability to tune into the mind of any person making a vibration. The music of

DeBussy and Delius, the words of Shakespeare, the poetry of Coleridge and Wordsworth have all got this presence if we tune into the minds which originated their works.

It was this same feeling I would get with the Guru. Should I go and see him to discover if I felt the same? I would go through the same anticipations of regret as I had done with Einstein. I was concerned that I should see him once again before he died. There were no works to relate to, no thoughts but only my own impressions of that period as a roaming sannyasin from 1960 to 1962.

This feeling had become very strong by the end of 1963 and I wrote the house in Calcutta for news of the Guru. They wrote back very strangely. "He talks all the time in strange sentences whilst in trance, but we cannot understand them," his family said. I thought what a pity I was not there, because some of his most mystifying speeches to me had contained the deepest wisdom. After I had unravelled the complexity of my own mind and I could see life simply, his words would often come crashing through my unconscious with always a double meaning hidden in them. I wanted to send a tape recorder to record these unintelligible words. Maybe he had gone crazy or senile or the words were jangled up in the stream of consciousness, but I was sure there were moments of extreme lucidity as there had been in my previous contact. But somehow I never got around to it and I was feeling the guilt of neglect.

In the year of 1964 I was doing a four-month tour on the road and I had just arrived in Los Angeles when someone suggested I meet Dr. Evarts Loomis who had a wholistic healing center in Hemet. We drove out to the desert which was being reclaimed with orange trees and stayed at the Center. Evarts and I got on very well and we walked round his property together nailing up "No Hunting" signs. The next day he suggested going to a certain Indian Rock for a meditation to experience the psychic atmosphere. We drove up to the wooded area of the mountains, passing through the small summer resort town of Idyllwild. Turning a corner Evarts suddenly remembered a spiritual friend who was also into meditation. He thought the more energy we had the better. Besides, he explained, this lady is a sculptor and is very psychic. He stopped outside a log cabin which acted as her shop and gallery. Evarts went in to see if she was in and I waited.

Jane Miller was a middle-aged mystic who I could see was surrounded by a very blue devotional aura. I noticed the statue of St. Francis she had carved in the garden. She came out with Evarts and we talked for a few minutes about attitudes to sculpture. I told her that I myself had owned a successful art gallery for several years and at this she mentioned that occasionally she did pastel drawings. She explained that this kind of drawing was untrained and was rather special because when she did a portrait, it was of the psychic being rather than the likeness. I began thinking, "Yes, a lot of artists rationalize this way when they cannot draw well enough to get a likeness." She invited me in to see her latest work but I was rather cool and suggested we go to Indian Rock for the meditation.

We sat at Indian Rock for about twenty minutes and we all felt a very high vibration mingling with our own intensity. It was a profound moment and we all three turned and looked into each other's eyes. Jane Miller looked at me and said, "You have an Indian teacher don't you?"

I said yes, not American Indian but in Calcutta.

She said, "I would like you to look at my latest work. I have been up most of the night doing it. It was very strange; I have never had any connection with the East but early

217

this morning I woke up about three a.m. and felt an irresistible urge to do a portrait. It was like a hand was guiding my own and I have never seen anyone like it in my life, so it could not be my unconscious. With your knowledge you might be able to tell me whether it's worth anything. Living these days hand-to-mouth off my works I have a hard time putting a value on things. Would you look at it?"

We reached the gallery down in the town again and got out of the car. Evarts and I followed her to the front door. Then, rather dramatically, she flung open the front door and said, "Come into my humble little log cabin," and stepped back for us to precede her down the entrance hall.

Imagine my shock when right on the wall opposite, within six feet of my nose, was a perfect portrait of the Guru in pastel colors. There was no mistaking it. He had a certain expression which he rarely showed anyone. But living with him for such a long time I had learnt every nuance of his personality. This was an expression of a certain frown with a look of sadness when people did not understand him or were especially obtuse. It was a deep expression of compassion mixed with some critical displeasure at the hopelessness of ever communicating his real Being. It was an expression he very rarely allowed to mar his all-joy Being. Most people would not even notice because it always was in contrast to his normal bubbling Self. I was flabbergasted at the likeness and stopped dead in my tracks.

"Where did you get that picture?" I asked, thinking she must have copied it from some photograph.

"That is the picture I was telling you about. It just came through my hands this very morning and I put it up there on the wall just before you came."

This is a photograph of the psychic portrait done by Jane Miller.

It was incredible. This feeling that I should go and visit the Guru had been gnawing away at my being, like it had with Einstein before, and now comes this picture out of the blue. I turned to Evarts who said, "I knew there was some strong reason for bringing you here to Indian Rock and my sudden impulse to bring Jane Miller was obviously no accident."

"What an incredible likeness!" I thought as I looked at the picture and here only moments ago I was doubting her ability to get a physical likeness, because most psychic artists are plain frauds. I had seen so many pastels of Indian guides, great deva spirits and so-called reincarnations which all looked alike that I had programmed that into our relationship when we first met. Here was a striking proof of telepathic contact.

I did not go to the Guru, so the Guru found me in a small tourist town amongst the pine trees of California. Here I was standing in front of the living image of the one man I should go and see again before he died. It was a subtle reproach that I had been so busy running around the world founding cultural centers, art galleries, small communities, etc., that I had no time left to come to the source, to dip into the deeper Self.

What was the message? Was he saying it's time to come? Or was he saying you cannot escape me even in the middle of the California desert? Or was he saying there is no need to come because I am coming to you?

Certainly the last alternative was true. He had the power to come to me through others when my own psychic awareness was too raced off its feet. I resolved to tune into the many people I was meeting and see if he was also acting through them. I was astonished when I thought of all the timing and manipulating which had to take place for someone to invite me to Hemet, then for Evarts in turn to invite me to Indian Rock and then for Jane Miller to sit down a few hours before to draw and then to invite us into her house. I did not doubt the Guru's samadhi after this but knew he had the power to stay in telepathic contact.

I had long given up the idea of owning things like paintings. I had been selling off my own art collection of West Indian painters and was unloading my collection as fast as I could to leading galleries and collectors, and the last thing I wanted to buy was a work of art, particularly one I had been asked to put a value on. How could I value this picture? It was a priceless example of telepathy, an incredible method of contacting anyone as well as an exact replica of a living person, as any of my photographs of the Guru could prove.

Something came over me. I would not own something I could get attached to, something that I could become obsessively possessive about. I asked Jane how much she would sell it for. She said, "I usually get $50 to $100 for a portrait but I leave the price to you if you want it." The thought struck me that if this was meant for me to own like a possession then it would be given, but because of Jane's financial need I felt she should get what she could for it. I could easily have paid $50 for it, but something said, "Once you put a price on it, the value of the message has gone." So I did what I had done with all my art collection and stood in front of it and photographed it in my head, burning the image into my imagination so strongly that it could not be taken away. When I had decided not to possess any work of art I had gone round all the leading museums of the world, stealing their great works in my head and storing them there with full recall of their clarity and beauty. I repeated the technique now, staring at every detail and every stroke of the crayon, noting the way the white hair whisped up just as it did around his face in real life.

We parted because we had already spent more time than intended. Evarts had a busy medical practice in Hemet and we had stolen time to come out to Idyllwild. I drove away and was quiet all the way back. I was thinking what a fantastic work of art is the mind of man that it can create works of beauty through others who are thousands of miles away from where they are sitting.

Several years later when I had moved my headquarters from my Blue Mountain laboratory to Centre House in London I had just come in from doing Christmas shopping when my wife handed me a cardboard roll and said, "This came in the mail for you today. Strange, there is no sender's name on the package." I thought it must be one of those calendars that people send at Christmas time and put it down to look at later when I was less busy.

It was Christmas day and we were all just opening our presents. The Community I had founded in London had finished a meditation together and then gathered round after breakfast to open our presents as a group. I went up from the dining room in the basement floor to the first floor where I kept my office and laboratory, to fetch some scissors to cut strings and open up the parcels. I noticed the tube lying on the office desk and cut off the end to see what was in it. I pulled out the piece of paper inside, wondering whatever it could be. When it rolled open I saw it was the portrait done by Jane Miller all those years ago. I had remembered every detail of it, burned into my brain with the fire of consciousness. A short note on a very small piece of paper fell out on the floor. I picked it up and read, "I think this really belongs to you. —Happy Christmas." No signature, no address.

LETTING GO

Does the universe out there exist
separate from the consciousness
which perceives it imprisoned in time?
From what immense longing
did its forces spring?
Somewhere in the vast, awesome
timeless beauty of it all
is the tenderness of the mother
and passion of the father
and the synthesis
of all else that we experience
in our consciousness.

He who can stand in the Holy place
and share the inspiration of God's Being
becomes the divine teacher
who brings beauty into the heart
and love into the eyes.

God uses the imagination and thought
of one who has no thoughts and images
of his own.
The all-knowing One pervades
the depths and heights of Being
when we are humble enough
to let go of all we know.

UNIVERSAL LOVE

Is real love emotional or devotional?

Do dimensions of love exist in nature
other than human emotion?
Does the dog who loves his master
understand the highest devotion?
Look deep into his eyes and see
the love untrammeled by human values,
that Pure love without thought,
the Pure love
which expects nothing in return,
the love that is selfless.
For Love is nothing but the attraction of the ONE
for its own Ultimate Self.

Is real love a powerful attraction
or an expansive radiation?
Does it suck you into the center,
or is it radiating you out?

In human terms the love that sucks you in
makes you a sucker.
The love that radiates you out
makes you a passionate giver.

Is real love powerful and aggressive?
Is it tentative, gentle?

Surrendering is sucking in and taking inwards.
Radiating and expanding is the power of giving outwards.

Both are equally aggressive and gentle.

Love is both functional and beautiful.
Your Love is your ultimate aggression;
use its passion gently in humility
before the wild union with the ONE.

All motion and vibration comes
out of the center of this Desire.
Two opposite forces,
male and female, positive and negative,
make up the evolutionary Desire for stillness
in all things.

Oneness of God asserts itself
when the generative desire causes inequality
between two opposites, male-female.
Desire is not quenched until the two forces
of surrender and projectivity are equal.

Light is the root of consciousness.
Consciousness is the by-product of Desire.
Desire stops when the ONE is found.
When ONE is found Desire becomes True Love.

True Love desires nothing but the seed
of all things.
The seed of all things is planted
in the whole of mankind.
The whole of man's desire is an effect
of the first cause.
The first cause is Desire to know
the complete self.

*KNOW THYSELF and thou shalt know
the depths of Desire.*

*Know thyself and know the annihilation
of Desire.*

*Know that the expansion of Light
is the desire to KNOW THYSELF.*

*Light and consciousness and desire
are ONE.*

THOU ART THAT ONE.

THE BLACK HOLE
OF CALCUTTA 19

Sitar

The real instrument is consciousness.

I was remembering how I had been travelling incognito from ashram to ashram for some weeks. Just quietly visiting some of India's well-known yogis and holymen and drinking in the spiritual atmosphere of India and looking at the manifestations, habits and disciples of gurus generally. I remembered feeling a special affinity for it all as if I had been there before.

Now, ten years later I had come back to the same old places which had such poignant memories for me, but it had all changed. Nothing was the same. Thousands of young Americans and Europeans were swarming everywhere, in the temples and juice bars and walking the bazaars in Indian clothes, but the atmosphere was not the same. India had changed and that spiritual quality that I had known and drunk deeply of as a sadhu all those years ago seemed to be missing. I began to wonder if it was I who had changed and become more cynical, less romantic, or whether these young people were experiencing what I felt was missing as still being there in some eternal way. Maybe they were tuning in to what had been in the past and savoring it like I had done. It was hard to be judgemental because some of the aspects of life in India were even more real. The poverty of Calcutta was now so acute that it was quite unsafe to walk the streets. Hundreds of murders, naxalite assassinations by political fanatics and robbings were taking place every day. I remembered well walking through the slums of Calcutta ten years before and tried to recall my experience as I watched the young people wander around today's version of India.

I remembered I had left the first holyman from Birla Temple back in Delhi in order to go down to Bombay and Madras and visit the Sri Aurobindo ashram in Pondicherry. My political friend in Delhi was the President of the World Union Movement founded upon the work of the great yogi Sri Aurobindo, so he wanted me to visit the shrine and meet the people who administered the ashram who were old colleagues of his. But after a while there I became anxious to meet the first holyman again because I had met several of the well-known great yogis of India and somehow they did not compare. I knew comparisons in the spiritual life of oneness were all odious but there was something uncanny and bizarre about the first one that seemed to add another dimension to life. There was a completely wild wisdom that did not come from any traditional source, did not trade off the heritage of thousands of years but seemed to have an original vibration.

The holyman had said he would be in Calcutta and had given me an address at Kalighat in the heart of the city alongside the famous temple built to Mother Kali, the devourer of hearts and souls. I took the flight from Madras to Calcutta and could not help feeling that this luxurious way of travelling would not be mine in the next two years to come. I had already had to travel several miles by bullock cart, hundreds of miles in crowded trains with standing room only, ridden on buses that were falling to pieces, and floated on rickety boats which crossed rivers. So at the airport I left my bags in check at the airline and decided to take a rattling tram car part of the way to Kalighat and walk the rest on foot. It was the best way to know this great city of 8 million souls.

Wandering through the streets of Calcutta was indeed an education in how the millions lived in poverty at the very edge of life and death. Dirt and filth were everywhere. Food was full of amoebic dysentery. Beggars were scratching in the gutters for carpenter's nails, bits of tin cans, wire off crates, the odd rusty screw, in fact, anything that could be sold for a few annas at the market. I wondered if the western nations ever realized that what they threw away was prized here as riches.

My heart was very heavy. How could there ever be beauty among so much filth? How could there be anything spiritual in the midst of so much dirt and disease? People just had no time left from scratching among the garbage to get on with the discipline of a spiritual life. How could they even think of spiritual things when their entire consciousness must be placed on survival and their dreams be only of the next meal?

Lepers and people with large swellings in the neck and sores on their backs rubbed shoulders in the milling crowds around the third class tea stands. I thought to myself, "Yes, I can buy some tea although I see it is made in a very dirty pan because it is actually boiled." The scare of catching the dreaded amoebic dysentery which I already had been ill with in Egypt and Pakistan was relieved by knowing that the milk and tea and water is boiled together and therefore, to my western mind, safe.

I knew one of every three Indians was a carrier of the amoebic strain and was immune because five out of every ten babies died with it and so if you pulled through you could live with it but never get rid of it. Its effects on the malnutritioned body were evident all around me. People had no energy, and life was listless in the midst of running rickshaws and a million bicycles. I watched the sordid scene and photographed all the suffering in my head. "How can there be beauty and spirit in all this?" my mind kept repeating.

I am walking now with all these thoughts crowding inside my head and sorrowful in my heart. How can the poor be helped? Every politician says he is out to help them but you get down to nitty-gritty with him it's the votes, the power structure and his own egotism which come first. Great schemes were all held up on the desks of men who wanted their slice in terms of power, influence or money.

The system was impenetrable and corruption subtle; even in the schemes for aiding the people the charity never reached the dregs of society for whom it is intended.

Walking amongst the terribly hungry and the dying corpses which just lie down in the gutter when their time has come, one gets a worm's eye perspective on the lives of so-called great men. The great personalities and names on the lips of all the great powers, the presidents and film stars and prominent spiritual leaders, what do they have to do with all this in their nice clean flowered churches every Sunday? And the ashrams all set out with flowers and the gurus seated on thrones of gold and silk, what do they have to offer life at this level? Could beauty exist amongst such ugliness or could a holyman detach from it in divine apathy? Could he look the other way, ignore what he was powerless to save and go his own sweet spiritual way, getting more disciples, more donations for more buildings to house more western disciples who were affluent. What did it all mean and who really cared?

As I walked through the day I came closer and closer to Kalighat. The poverty got worse and I began to wonder if this holyman was really a great man if he lived in a part of Calcutta with such squalor. Where was the music of life, the beauty of spirit, the joy of a life well lived?

I looked around me and compared the Indian attitude of leaving everything to karma, to fate, and the Christian ethic of serving man, of doing good to those who are poor, of starting hospitals for the sick, dormitories for those who are destitute. I noticed that most of the private hospitals in India organized by charity were either run by Christian nuns or missionaries. I began to question the spirituality of these great gurus as I walked along and thought surely there must be a blend of Christ and Krishna. Could there ever be a change in attitudes? What a change it would have to be!—from sitting glorified by disciples on thrones like small popes dispensing blessings to the devout while most of the newly born millions die slowly in the gutters of the world.

I had offered India a scheme for feeding its millions from the sun's light. It had been tested in Japan and could work. By growing certain edible strains of algae, thousands of acres of rice fields could produce forty tons of food instead of four. The Prime Minister Mr. Nehru had given it top priority with the Ministry of Agriculture; the minister was thrilled with the idea and already the politicians had seen it as a way of controlling the people's votes—with food. Yet the signs were there as I walked through the valley of death in Calcutta that they who needed would never see any of it. Even the 250 million cows of India would never see any of it though it could keep the whole cow population off the land. In that way the people could use the land for growing other foods.

I did not know then that the project would be approved as priority number one by three more Prime Ministers. Many times it would be submitted to governments, and years later I would abandon it, still stuck on the desks of the officials who thought they knew some other friends who could get the grants, or still stuck in the minds of those who saw opportunity for selfish ambition and enormous wealth in the green gold that was going to flow from the sun's light.

Unconsciously I must have known all this as I walked in the slums of Calcutta and realized the situation was hopeless, that big schemes for saving man could not be achieved by little minds of men. But we could not be found wanting by not trying, by not caring, by not doing. Until we changed men from the inside I could see clearly that giving them material affluence, first in food and then all the gadgets, would achieve nothing. Mankind could only be as it really is, and it could not act with any greater wisdom or selflessness than the highest state of social human consciousness. Yet this dictum itself often repeated by Communists, was false too, because the social consciousness is not some abstract idea in the head or some legislated idealistic dogma, but made up of the spiritual insights of each person like you and me. We could not look at it separately from ourself, then shrug our shoulders and give up on it, because who is society? It is me and you and will not improve unless you and I improve it. To abdicate spiritual responsibility for it, was to surrender man's soul to the materialists, the atheists who believed only in political power and the supreme coercion of the state as an instrument of change. Something had to be done, but what? Did the gurus really have any answers sitting on their thrones repeating the scriptures ad nauseum?

All these thoughts ran through my head and sorrowed my heart as I picked my way through street after street of rotting humanity. How could one bring beauty and truth of life into such a black hole as Calcutta? Was it to be walking in hell, tortured by thoughts of impotence and inadequacy to meet this awesome challenge? How could anyone do anything with the resources of one puny little earth man? Why even United Nations and the big governments with millions were failing every day, and great organized charities were spending sixty-five percent of what they got from people's pockets to pay for staff and advertising costs. How could any one man do anything?

These were the thoughts in my head and with hurting heart I was walking like a mad Englishman in the midday sun of Calcutta all afternoon, when I could have been anywhere else in the world. I could have been meditating overlooking the temple at Delphi in the idyllic setting among the olive groves of Greece. I could have been sitting at home with my children on the beaches of the blue Caribbean watching them play. I could have been with the wife whose eyes had always shone with selfless love, whom I had left behind to selfishly seek the source of my own soul. I could have been preaching a fulfilling philosophy to the youth of my own country as I did later on; but at this moment I was in the smelly depths of the world's worst city, walking amongst the hopeless derelicts of life, feeling the flow of love for the ugly and the diseased brothers and sisters milling in the crowds around me.

This was no dream and the suffering pain of the many was felt by the One, that One who was in me and around me in the dirty streets of Calcutta as I came near to the house where the Guru lived among all this throbbing life of the humble and lost. Why did he do this? This man who could have lived anywhere, who would have been welcomed in Maharajah's palaces and talked with Presidents and spoke with the authority of kings.

I had been lost in my thoughts for hours as I walked aimlessly, and the evening light was failing. I remember asking someone how far was this address. He seemed to know the house well and said it was just around the corner, near the temple—not far to go. I relaxed and noticed it was the witching hour when everything seems to stand still as the darkness falls and the smell of jasmine perfume permeates the air. The streets suddenly became deserted as if everyone were inside meditating. The smell of dirt and the agonizing sights of the suffering seemed to disappear.

I paused and looked up and down the empty street and at that moment a sitar started to play the most haunting evening raga which wafted from the house I happened to have stopped at. It was incredibly beautiful and I stood transfixed savoring every moment, every note, and the poignant sense of resting in its beauty. I knew whoever was playing was playing to no audience but God. And I knew that God was listening to the musician's meditation through me. I stood without even moving a muscle for half an hour. Occasionally I felt someone pass by on their way down the street and they must have wondered or have known what I was doing. From the depths of hell I was delivered into Bliss. I could no longer feel my body, and my heart was on fire with the meditator's love of God. My fire answered his fire and although he did not know I was standing outside his little house, we had become one.

I was tempted to go down the path to the house when the raga finished and see what kind of mortal could play like that, but it was dark now so I went around the corner to look for the Guru's house and found it was very near. I walked up to the door and was admitted by a very sweet looking lady who took me into a large room where the Guru was sitting. He introduced me to what must have been his wife before he went to Mount Kailas and became a seer.

"Now," he said, "I shall introduce you to my daughter who will sing for you." I still did not know if he meant his real daughter because all girls were often called his daughter, but on this occasion I got the feeling she was his own blood.

I asked rather timidly, "Is this your real daughter?"

He said, "Yes, I have two daughters and both are doctors. One is a Doctor of Music and the other a Doctor of Sociology."

He called out a name and out came a very slender girl who looked about thirty. He asked her to bring her sitar and play a raga for me before she sang. She sat against the far wall of the room while the Guru and I sat in the middle of the floor to listen. I closed my eyes while she was tuning her strings. I was thinking of the raga which I had just heard around the corner of the block and I thought, "No one could play as well as that. What a pity I will have to listen to this Guru's daughter play after such a divine experience from an unknown master of meditation and the sitar. What a comparison I will be making."

I opened my eyes when she stopped tuning and watched as she smiled to me and then closed her eyes in meditation. Then she started to play the identical raga that I had just heard less than half an hour before in exactly the same way. I was mystified and entranced at the same time. It was fantastic and unbelievable, a dream all over again. Could this have been the same player whose sound floating out over the night air had made me one with God? There could be no mistake; it was identical! She must have been at the back of the house which stretched through to the other side of the block around the corner. What beauty and what power such music had to lift the human heart into other realms of Being.

Then she sang in Khyal style a well-known song and looked at me meaningfully as she was singing. I had the impression she knew I had been listening before in the oasis of spirit in this desert of suffering humanity. Perhaps the aroma of Being and the greatness of spirit of just a few who lived amongst the poor and hopeless sick of the world was the stuff that kept the great sprawling city of Calcutta alive. Perhaps without this beauty, life would have no meaning and Kali would indulge her ravenous appetite for human blood.

In that dream setting I felt an irresistible urge to run around the block and check out if it was real—whether that little house I had stood outside transfixed for half an hour in Bliss was really the back of this house. I resolved to look the next morning but at this moment the world was all one, it did not matter, it was all within the One and the player and listener were all one.

How incredible, I thought in my meditation that night, that only this afternoon I was asking myself how any lover of beauty and truth could exist amidst so much dirt and amongst so much suffering. How could one watch people slowly die in the gutters and within the hour be in Cosmic Bliss? Life was indeed a dream and the radiant joy of the Guru's face was not only as beautiful as his daughter's music, but seemed to be a triumph of love over death, a symbol of the ever living love that lies like a hidden secret in every suffering heart.

THE CELESTIAL SONG

The Divine sun sings its one song
through a billion billion atoms of Self,
and a billion billion atoms dance
to the celestial song.
The celestial song of Self is self-sung,
and heard only by the One I love.
All creation sings to the One
who hears itself sing
in the silence of the secret cave
of the heart.
Poets speak of bubbling joy
and musicians seek the signature of immortal song
to catch the spirit making love with supreme self
becoming One.
Yet a hymn to the spirit
in praise of essence
is not the sweetness of the song itself.
The poet's song is made of words;
like clumsy mittened hands
they grope for bliss.
God's song pierces the heart,
for the song is written not in words
but in joy.
Who can know the celestial song?
Only the one who sings it.
For the song of self is self-sung,
the effulgent light of all creation.
Poets praise and preachers preach,
and guru's mantram of a holy name
is supposed to flip you out
but it doesn't.
Joy and bliss are only words
until the active Cosmic Being
radiates love's essential nature
and passionately sings the celestial song.

DARKNESS INTO LIGHT

Sisters and brothers in the one Self,
have you forgotten
the message of the ultimate All?

When circumstances of life
confront our desires,
when the authorities around us
create intolerable situations,
when cosmic forces work
to darken the light of consciousness,
then it is time to see
> *the evil as good*
> *the wrong as right*
> *and the dark as light.*

The black hole
is bottomless endless awareness of all power
crushing light into dark singularity
and wrong into right
united in one common ground
of undivided being.

What is life's message
given from the singleness
of the ONE Force
which none can change?

*If you look for what is **not***
in the absolute
*and see **not** what is there,*
then the absolute reality annihilates
whatever the mind opposes,
for divisiveness
is a mind divided against itself.
Rigidity of mind does not exist
in the absolute One.

Life opposes death and brittleness,
tragedy opposes the comic fantasies
of pastel and sugary blue birds
going tweet tweet.
Happy endings are opposed
by painful beginnings,
and our expectations demand
that God care.
Should a black hole's enormous appetite for light
care for what it feeds upon?

The Cosmos limits us to what is.

Relationships are formed from what is limited,
and ideals are formed from what is not;
therefore destroy expectations
and give up ideals,
confront the universe in us
and see the ONE in darkness.

DEATH
*(Written in meditation two hours before learning
of my father's death.)*

*Death of body and senses causes
death of the mind and conscious memory
but the soul records the essence
of our evolution.
Out of this essence
conscious body and mind is born again and again.
The divine spark we call a soul
is pure consciousness
programmed with the cosmic record
of all our thoughts and actions.*

*The dead are asleep to this world of sensation
but they will awake and renew their earthly existence
in human form.
Sleep is but an inward breath of consciousness
which restores the soul,
and awakening is but an outward breath
of radiation from the center.*

*Life is a pendulum swing between
sleeping and waking, death and rebirth,
but the swing is circular not back and forth.
Therefore the beginning of one swing
is the end of another.*

*Death begins at the moment of birth.
Death is but a sleep and a forgetting,
but as we awake daily
renewed by sleep,
so do we awake totally renewed in body at birth.
Regeneration of the individual soul
is like the shedding of the snake's skin,
the new one has been slowly renewing itself beneath.*

Reincarnation is the putting on
of a new suit of clothes made of those small
crystals of matter we call the living flesh.

All things are continuously becoming and being.
All things sleep in death and awake in life!

All things that vibrate with life
return to that ONE
who lives eternally in stillness.
In the stillness of Death
is found the inner Peace of a life well lived.

In a life well lived,
at peace with all of creation
Death is no spectre to be feared.
It is a release
and a lightness of the Spirit
that no longer needs
the heaviness of the gross body.

Some die well and know
that they go home to the eternal ONE.
Some die clinging to life.
Some die in the midst of joy and laughter.
The few who know the stillness
of peace in life
welcome Death as we would welcome
sleep after a long day.

When we awake from Death
may we be given a new life of understanding.
May the True essence of our Soul remember
our gentleness and moments of sweetness.
May our next birthing bring us face to face
with THAT ONE who is our Father.

THE FINAL
MESSAGE

20

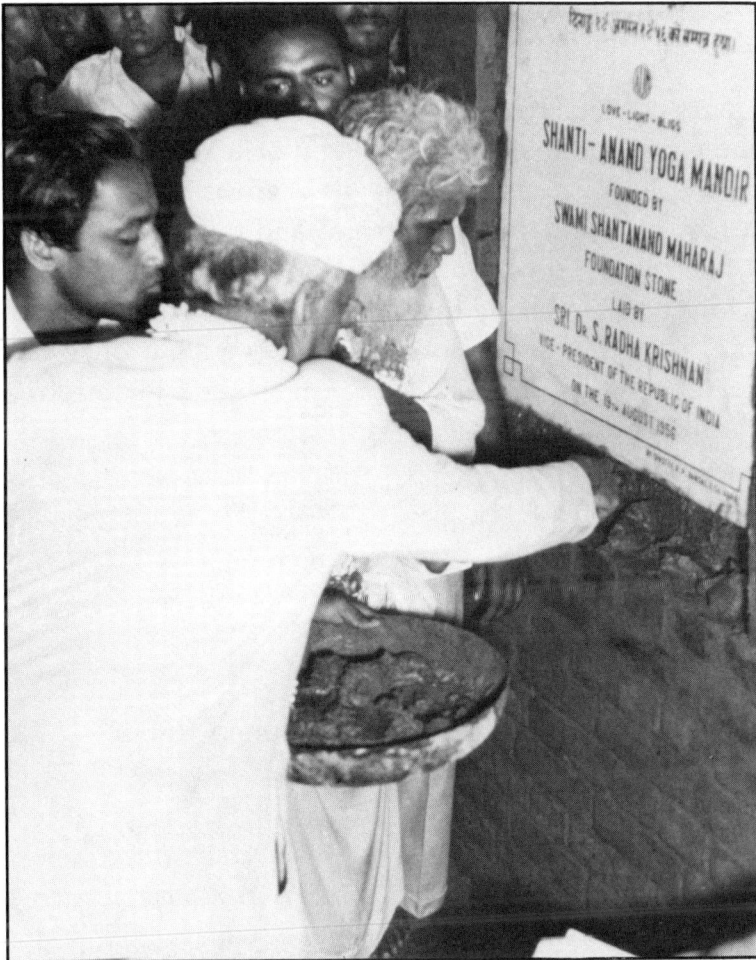

1956—The Guru and the Vice-President of India officially laid the
foundation stone of the World Yoga University. Sarvapalli Radha Krishnan,
the greatest interpreter of Indian philosophy, became President of India on the
retirement of President Rajendra Prasad.

I was high above the North Pole flying from Moscow to
New Delhi and my mind went back 10 years, remembering
the strange incident in a small ashram in Brindaban. The
ashram was at a place not far from where Krishna was
born and so all the gurus had ashrams there. I had been
travelling India as a sadhu for over a year and my Guru
had taken me to see Ma Ananda Mayi in Brindaban.
Suddenly he announced we would go to his own ashram
while we were in town. He had never even told me he
had an ashram there.

He marched through the gate and it was Bhajan time;
a whole group of people were singing Hari Krishna around
an altar with pictures of all the great gurus on it. When
they saw him they rushed forward and touched his feet
and then we sat down in the open near a big stone. We
had formed a circle and the Guru was answering questions
when I noticed that set in the stone was a big bronze plate
with some letters on it. I read in English and in Sanskrit
the words

> WORLD YOGA UNIVERSITY
> Foundation Stone
> Laid by Sarva Palli Radhakrishnan,
> Vice-President of India

and a date about 2 years before.

"What's that?" I said, "a foundation stone without
a building?"

"Yes," he said, "one day there will be a World Yoga
University."

I thought how arrogant to put the stone first without any
money to build the rest. I looked at him and said, "Who
will build it?"

"You will," he said briefly.

I laughed to myself. Me, build someone else's dream place? Not likely. I have enough ideas of my own to manifest.

Ten years later, here was I on my way back to meet with members of an institute I had founded for spiritual research with some friends of the Prime Minister Nehru. They had offered to finance a world conference, so I had ransacked my London files and put together a steering committee of important politicians and some cabinet ministers of the Indian government. They had offered a government grant because yoga was one of India's greatest invisible exports.

I had sent my young son ahead and for a whole year he travelled the ashrams of India getting the swamis and pundits to break an ancient tradition of seclusion and non-involvement in political affairs. This World Yoga Conference was to be a national event with all the top brass of the Indian philosophical and spiritual life involved in the steering committee.

Here I was ten years later, and guess what the theme of the conference was? "A World Yoga University." I had completely forgotten about that funny stone in a funny little ashram. The steering committee had surprisingly elected me President of the conference and given me the title of Acharya. The plane was almost there as I remembered this.

By the time I arrived all the difficulties in the world were flying in the teeth of this huge conference. With 50 Western scientists arriving for it at my own personal invitation, the conference had become a political football. The steering committee wanted to cancel.

Many of the Westerners and scientists were already on their way and could not be contacted. Almost 800 yogis from around the world had agreed to attend and 240 had submitted papers. At this late hour I had to assume full

Smoothing out a problem at the Conference.

My son John (to my right) helped to organize the Conference. Dr. Rammurti Mishra (second from the right in the photograph) was a frequent lecturer at my Centre in London.

246

One of India's finest dancers gave the conference an aesthetic dimension.

responsibility financially, and organizationally. I had to get rid of a useless steering committee that was fighting itself in a fashion better suited to the Mafia than a government-sponsored group of yoga enthusiasts. Fortunately, none of the politicians were yogis and so they were left alone and the yogis banded together behind me to make the conference work.

People appeared from out of nowhere to offer help. Westerners with degrees in Sanskrit flew down from Nepal, hippies from the beaches of India came to help put up the big demonstration tents and many wonderful people gave me moral support to continue in the face of continuous political maneuvers by the steering committee to wreck the conference with their divisiveness. It felt as though a great ship was being rocked in a violent sea of psychic forces, and all the highly developed egos were bristling like a bunch of porcupines. Many times I felt those forces from powerful people who, for some reason, wanted the conference to fail.

The day of inauguration came and at 9 a.m. on 20th December 1970 an old friend and colleague who was Chairman of the Department of Indian Religion and Philosophy at Benares Hindu University was giving the opening speech. It was touch and go as there were fanatical religio-political factions threatening to wreck the huge conference with demonstrations behind the scenes.

I wished I could have got away from it all. The pressure and responsibility was getting to me and I wanted to go to Calcutta to see my Guru whom I had not seen for nearly 10 years. I had thought of going to see him before the conference but immediately on arrival I had been sucked into this whirling controversy over who would share the power and imaginary political profits of the conference.

248

I was in a state of numbed acceptance wondering what would happen next.

As if by some superior magic an invisible hand seemed to guide the huge conference like a lumbering elephant through a whole mass of complicated changes. The conference ticked away and mysteriously became a huge success. I could not believe how well things were going. Even at the last session in the huge Government Hall when I had to cut short a boisterous so-called yogi from Germany who was trying to dispute a statement in one of my published books that Christ was a yogi, it was done with so much good humor that I wondered if we would get through to the 7:00 p.m. closing time without some horrific incident.

My reserves of energy had been sucked away by the constant need to be everywhere amongst the seven conference streams running concurrently together. There was only one hour to go and I expressed the idea to an Indian member of my committee that I would like to finish on time.

"Finish on time is impossible in India," he shouted in my ear above the din of the microphones. He said that in India these public events do not go according to the clock, even though the conference had gone along on time during the four days. "That was a miracle," he said.

Just at that moment I was called away to the side of the public platform for an urgent phone call from Calcutta. They had been trying to get to me for four days. I picked up the phone and a voice said, "I am speaking for Guru Shantananda Maharaj. Are you Acharya Christopher Hills?"

"Yes, I am he," I said, thrilled at the thought of speaking to the Guru and telling him I would be over to Calcutta as soon as I could leave. I had planned taking a party of twenty-three people around the spiritual shrines of India immediately after the conference and I was anxious for them to meet the Guru who was the most loveable person I had ever met.

"Hello, are you there?" the voice said.

"Yes, go ahead."

"I have a message for you from Guruji. He said to be sure and tell you to finish on time because some religious fanatics have planned to shoot some of the swamis on the platform, including yourself, about 8:00 p.m. at night."

"How do you know this?" I asked. Calcutta was three days train ride away from Delhi.

"Just a message we have been trying to give you for four days but we could not get you on the phone."

I looked at my watch. It was 10 minutes to go to official closing time. An unheard of thing in India would be to close at the stated time. I asked, "Can I speak to Guruji please?"

"That is not possible. He is not alive."

"What!" I gasped. "When did he die?" The answer came as an even bigger shock, for I had not let anyone in Calcutta know of the final details of the conference.

"At 9:00 a.m. on the 20th December Guruji died."

I made a mental note of the time as I made my way hurriedly back to the stage. At that exact time four days ago I was just completing my introduction of the inaugurator of the conference. My Guru had died while I was speaking to the yogis assembled from all over the world. "How strange," I thought, "to die at that moment."

My thoughts were confused, I was responsible for this huge conference and at this last session the public had been invited so I returned to the platform in New Delhi's largest concert hall, the Vigyan Bhavan. Before me were nearly 3,000 people, all interested in the spiritual science of yoga.

I looked at my watch as the last speaker completed his speech. It was five minutes to seven. If I let another speaker go on we would surely go past seven. I took the microphone in my hand and stood in silence for a moment before announcing that, as advertised, the conference would finish on time at 7:00 p.m. and then I was asking one of the swamis to chant the closing OM.

Even while the OM was being sounded there was an uproar, as several people struggled to get on the stage to grab the microphones. One succeeded in getting to the stand and started talking like a politician with his eyes all inflamed with passion and hatred. I went up to the mike and wrenched the wire out of its socket.

The conference was over. If anyone was going to shoot now there were over a hundred people swarming on the stage. It was impossible to move. The conference was over. I went out the stage backdoor and looked at the stars.

"How bizarre life is," I thought. And even in death my Guru had been totally unpredictable. It could not have been coincidence for him to die at the moment of my own fulfillment as the president of a worldwide yoga conference dedicated to founding a World Yoga University.

Looking at the stars and at the height of fame, I felt saddened that I had not seen the Guru before his death. It had been close on 10 years since we roamed India together as a pair of wandering mendicant sannyasins.

251

Memories flooded back of other bizarre times. It was too much love to bear. I decided to become a recluse as soon as my commitments were completed.

But God had other plans for me. Shortly after the conference I was offered several sites for the University by rich men with crores of rupees to build it where they wanted it to be. But my thoughts went back to Brindaban and that rock inscription. What did I need a Yoga University for? I wanted to be as free as my Guru, and this project would tie me to a role, an accepted position, and I would have no time for seclusion.

I began to experience a sense of freedom. We don't have to do what is expected of us by others, but we have to be true to ourselves to find the love and purity of God's grace. My spirit, which had been weighed down with all its duties and the self-important role of President and organizer, suddenly felt light and free and soaring whenever I looked at the night sky. Where was the spirit of the Guru in the vast expanse of the cosmos? What did it all mean? What had happened to all the work and expense for Universal Government, world government and the Yoga University now that the 800 yogis of the conference had voted for it?

I found myself laughing inside. What did a yogi need a university for when he had the whole universe spinning in his consciousness? To be able to close one's eyes and soar to the edges of the universe in pure space and catch that incredibly clever Guru by the tail and to be free reminded me of a saying of an ancient Chinese sage:

> A bird leaves no traces
> as it flies through space.
> The perfect runner
> leaves no tracks.

The way of the universe
is mysterious and unfathomable
and yet it is intelligent.

I was back at square one again, a different person in
the same body. Something was pulling me away from yogis
and their desire for students. Something was pulling me
away from conferences and away from human concepts of
how things should be done. Would the desperately hungry
world be fed by any known techniques of food production?
Would man reach universal salvation by any particular
religion or system? Would I be fulfilled or could I help
anyone else to be fulfilled by following any long tradition?

These thoughts kept coming at me from out of the night
sky. Somewhere up there and out through space, the
Universal One was being born in countless beings. It
was being reborn in me in no particular form or shape,
with no particular philosophy except that consciousness
itself was all there is. It was one and it was love. Not love
of anything in particular but just the vibration of love—
a sweet love that reminded me of my Guru's shining face
and the twinkle in his eyes. At the end of it all it was
just a subtle twinkle that made the difference between
a life well lived and a life of heaviness and too much care.

I thought of the Guru again and again and realized he
had died of too much love. Was it possible to be born
with too much love? Did some people have so much that
they had to give away the surplus to keep themselves sane?

Every time I look at the night sky with the vault of heaven
as my cathedral roof, the words come to me: "God created
the universe out of too much love." My heart begins to
ache and my body feels light and the spirit soars and I
think of the One I love.

BOOKS BY CHRISTOPHER HILLS

Published or Distributed by University of the Trees Press
P.O. Box 66
Boulder Creek, California 95006

Christ-Yoga of Peace

Christopher Hills offers a deep vision of human potential for selfgoverning communities where people can live together in harmony and peace and where leadership can flower within each person. Not a mere utopian concept, but a practical constitution for making it happen, first in small groups and organizations and then expanding to larger communities.

The Christ Book

The Christ Book is a transcription of talks Christopher Hills gave in response to questions from many people who wanted to apply Christ's teachings to practical, real-life situations, such as relationships, marriage, fidelity, money, power, romance, love, healing and true spirituality. Beautifully illustrated, *The Christ Book* has a wonderful power to touch and respond to a reader's deepest questionings, bringing alive the 2,000 year old message with penetrating insight, and bringing one closer to a personal relationship with Christ.

Course in Direct Perception

A profound 3-year course of study that takes you step by step to your own enlightenment. Learn to pray and meditate scientifically through meditation on the words of Christ and experience directly for yourself the same essence of clear perception taught by all the great world religions.

Creative Conflict: Learning to Love with Total Honesty

Creative Conflict not only describes the right role that conflict can play in human relationships and in the world arena, but shows you how to make all your inner and outer conflicts into creative opportunities for dynamic spiritual growth. In human relations a bond of closeness is born when conflict is truly resolved. The techniques and methods for Creative Conflict outlined by Christopher Hills do not involve compromise but a willingness to get to the greatest truth that considers all points of view. If you have not tried it you cannot imagine what a tremendous effect Creative Conflict can have on the quality of life.

Exploring Inner Space

Practical activities, awareness exercises and games to explore and experience each of seven levels of consciousness together with friends and family. Find out more about who you really are and deepen your relationships and communication with others.

Food From Sunlight

A scientific book on how to grow algae with charts and figures as well as the history of Dr. Hills and Dr. Nakamura's efforts in algae production. Also outlines their efforts to reveal the potential of Chlorella and Spirulina algae for feeding the hungry world.

Friday Night Taped Lecture Series "Questions from the Heart"

Inspirational talks given by Christopher Hills in answer to deep questions from the lives of many individuals that have arisen out of their spiritual search. A complete catalog of these taped programs is available from the publisher.

The Golden Egg
A no-holds-barred look from a rare spiritual vantage point at the economic realities of the world today and the choices before governments which will shape our material destiny. *The Golden Egg* offers practical alternatives to get off the wheel of inflation-recession and big government deficits by going to the spiritual and fundamental causes behind the problems that are far deeper than current economic theories indicate. Christopher Hills also presents guidelines on how to spiritualize your own economic or business life so that you will have real security.

Joy of Slimming
The spiritual approach to weight loss and better health, this book combines Christopher Hills' insights into the attitudes that keep people overweight, and shows you how to change your mental appetite as well as your physical cravings.

Imprisoned Light
A short and concise book of facts on Spirulina that answers many common questions about the nutritional properties of this miraculous and wonderful helical algae found at the primal base of the food chain, grown from sunlight and water.

Secrets of the Life Force
A book on ancient Egypt and a scientific understanding of the life force and how the Egyptians were able to harness it, and how you, too, can experiment with the Egyptian methods in modern times.

Supersensonics: The Science of Radiational Paraphysics
The results of over twenty years of scientific research, *Supersensonics* displays the genius of Christopher Hills' mind in discovering and demonstrating a way of sensing and measuring the subtle vibratory planes of consciousness, including thought, energy, electromagnetic and life-force fields in the pre-matter state. Explains why water dowsing works and discusses the universal field searched for in vain by Einstein.

Nuclear Evolution
Christopher Hills' in-depth study of the nature and structure of human consciousness is found in this 1,000 page masterpiece that unites physics, psychology and religion by showing how light and consciousness are one and the same, and how the human personality absorbs and re-radiates light through seven prismatic filters. *Nuclear Evolution* uncovers the potential waiting to be discovered within each soul, and helps you to identify and unfold through color psychology, seven different levels of consciousness within yourself that make you who you are.

Rejuvenating the Body
A complete, easy to follow program to cleanse the body and renew health and well-being. Spirulina is a fantastic "super" food researched for twenty years by Christopher Hills as a means to alleviate world hunger. This high protein algae, one of the most primitive life forms available as food, is shown as an excellent aid to your total health program.

Rise of the Phoenix
In all of his writings, Christopher Hills points to the potential of each person to glorify our Creator, the Divine Love and Intelligence, and to bring that divinity into each human being. This awakening is the Rise of the Phoenix, the soul within, out of the ashes of our limited ego-confined personalities, into the light of full realization. Awesome and inspiring, this book offers a sobering vision of humanity's choices and the role each one of us must play to make sure that choice is for the fullest unfoldment of life, love and light.

Science of Vibration and Transmission of Life Force
This course of study of twenty-four taped sessions expands your consciousness beyond its present mental and physical limits. Experience the Oneness realized by Christopher Hills by developing your own imagination and intuition to perceive the subtle spiritual vibrations of life, essential for pure love, pure wisdom and pure consciousness.

Success is a Way of Life
A wonderful and inspiring pocket book on how to become successful on all seven levels of our personal lives—including spiritually, emotionally, intellectually, socially and monetarily. One of Christopher Hills' simplest and most direct books, yet filled with his unparalleled wisdom, spoken by a man who has attained what he promises to others who follow his recipe for total success.

Spiritual Diary and Appointment Calendar
365 quotations from the works of Christopher Hills make this spiritual diary a deep well of inspiration. They keep you tuned to your own highest potential. An inspirational gift for the bedside.

For more information on these and other fine books, tapes and tools of perception, write:

UNIVERSITY OF THE TREES PRESS
P.O. Box 66
Boulder Creek, California 95006